Beginning Radio Communications

Radio Projects and Theory

Alex Wulff

Apress®

Beginning Radio Communications: Radio Projects and Theory

Alex Wulff
Cambridge, MA, USA

ISBN-13 (pbk): 978-1-4842-5301-4   ISBN-13 (electronic): 978-1-4842-5302-1
https://doi.org/10.1007/978-1-4842-5302-1

Managing Director, Apress Media LLC: Welmoed Spahr
Acquisitions Editor: Aaron Black
Development Editor: James Markham
Coordinating Editor: Jessica Vakili

Cover designed by eStudioCalamar

Cover image designed by Freepik (www.freepik.com)

Distributed to the book trade worldwide by Springer Science+Business Media New York, 233 Spring Street, 6th Floor, New York, NY 10013. Phone 1-800-SPRINGER, fax (201) 348-4505, e-mail orders-ny@springer-sbm.com, or visit www.springeronline.com. Apress Media, LLC is a California LLC and the sole member (owner) is Springer Science + Business Media Finance Inc (SSBM Finance Inc). SSBM Finance Inc is a **Delaware** corporation.

For information on translations, please e-mail rights@apress.com, or visit http://www.apress.com/rights-permissions.

Apress titles may be purchased in bulk for academic, corporate, or promotional use. eBook versions and licenses are also available for most titles. For more information, reference our Print and eBook Bulk Sales web page at http://www.apress.com/bulk-sales.

Any source code or other supplementary material referenced by the author in this book is available to readers on GitHub via the book's product page, located at www.apress.com/978-1-4842-5301-4. For more detailed information, please visit http://www.apress.com/source-code.

Printed on acid-free paper

I dedicate this book to my family—their unwavering support in all my endeavors means the world to me.

Table of Contents

About the Author

Alex Wulff is a maker and student of electrical engineering at Harvard. Alex has always had a passion for sharing his love of technology with the world and has given numerous talks encouraging youth and adults alike to get involved with the maker movement. He has a special interest in radio technologies and their increasingly important role in today's connected society.

Alex is very active in the maker community and posts a variety of projects online. To see his work, visit `www.AlexWulff.com/go`

CHAPTER 1

Introduction and Materials

Communication is perhaps the most import tool in humanity's toolbox. Without it, the scope and depth of the human race's ambition would be vastly limited. New means of communication precipitated important milestones in our time on this planet. Radio waves allowed for the first wireless communications, then gave us broadcasting of news, music, and entertainment. It is radio communications that carry us into a new age of global connectivity, allowing billions of devices to communicate with one another.

Without radio technologies, space travel, cell phones, satellite Internet, and many other technologies we take for granted would be next to impossible. Radio waves are comprised of electromagnetic radiation, which travels at the speed of light. Until humanity expands its communications into the quantum realm, the speed of light remains the fastest speed at which humans can transmit information.

With this text, you will gain an intuitive understanding of how humans have harnessed radio waves to achieve light-speed communication across vast distances. Everything from how radio waves propagate to how information is encoded and transmitted is covered. We'll also discuss specific communications systems and how they operate. Throughout the text, you'll get the opportunity to put your skills into practice with real communications systems and hardware. In one exercise, you'll use a

© Alex Wulff 2019
A. Wulff, *Beginning Radio Communications*,
https://doi.org/10.1007/978-1-4842-5302-1_1

software-defined radio (SDR) to download images from weather satellites. In another, you'll use microcontrollers and radio modules to send packets of data back and forth. In yet another exercise, you'll use a satellite to talk with individuals up to a thousand miles away.

A large portion of this text is devoted to amateur radio, or "ham radio" as it's popularly known. Amateur radio is a global community of licensed radio operators—this book will show you how to get licensed, and help you learn how to use amateur radio hardware.

The purpose of this text is not to provide you with a complete and in-depth picture of a particular element of radio communications. Rather, this text is designed to give you an intuitive understanding of various important concepts in radio communications and how they fit into the larger picture. By understanding propagation of radio waves, you'll be able to deduce how various obstacles will affect the path of communications. By understanding different types of antennas, you'll be able to identify an antenna structure out in the world and determine its use. By understanding modulation and how information is encoded in radio waves, you can look at a communications protocol and surmise how it works. This text will give you the information necessary to form a natural understanding of the preceding topics, in addition to many more.

Materials

This is, by nature, a hands-on text. As such, you'll need to purchase some materials to complete the demonstrations and exercises. I recommend purchasing this hardware now so you have it when you need it later on in the book, even if you don't get around to using it for a while. Each item is listed under the chapter in which it is required.

Chapter 4: Project: Satellite Imagery

This is the first chapter in which materials are required. The purpose of this chapter is to utilize a device called a software-defined radio to download live images from a US weather satellite. Without the software-defined radio, you'll have no way to download data!

Software-Defined Radio Kit

Think of a software-defined radio as similar to a radio tuner like the one on your car. It can analyze incoming radio waves of a user-selectable frequency and output this information in a variety of ways. We will be using this particular kit to pick up transmissions from satellites as well as listen to people talk on the air.

The actual software-defined radio (SDR) is a small dongle that plugs into a USB-A port on a computer. Also included in this kit are all the antennas, mounts, and cables necessary for all the projects using the SDR. This software-defined radio is shown in Figure 1-1.

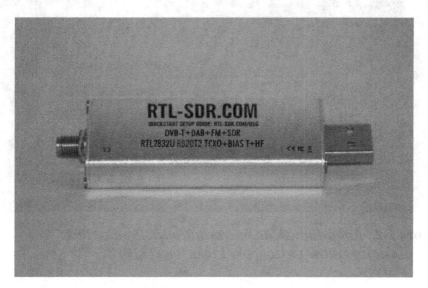

Figure 1-1. The RTL-SDR device. Product link: *www.alexwulff.com/ radiobook/links/sdr ($30)*

3

Chapter 6: Exploring Radio

In this chapter, you'll explore modern radio communications through a device called a microcontroller, as well as an inexpensive radio module.

Microcontroller (Arduino Uno)

The topic of microcontrollers is explained more in Chapter 6, but for now you can think of them as miniature computers. We will use this particular microcontroller to interface with the radio module. Such a microcontroller is shown in Figure 1-2.

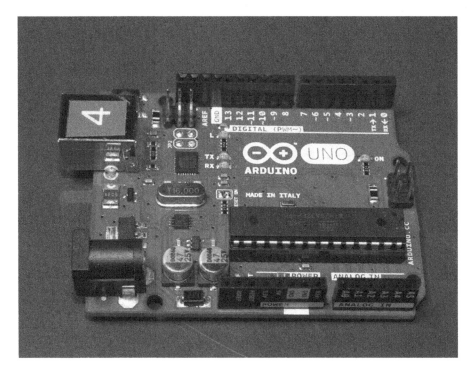

Figure 1-2. An Arduino Uno microcontroller. Product link: www.alexwulff.com/radiobook/links/uno ($17)

Radio Module (NRF24L01)

This radio module is what actually takes the data from the microcontroller and sends it via radio waves. It's easy to send data between these radio modules, and they're inexpensive, so they make great modules for educational purposes. The actual module itself is shown in Figure 1-3.

Figure 1-3. *The NRF24L01 radio module. Product link:*
www.alexwulff.com/radiobook/links/radiomodule ($12)

Male to Female Jumper Wires

Jumper wires are simply copper wires with a standardized connector on each end. One end of these wires plugs into the metal pins coming from the radio module, and the other plugs into the microcontroller. The alternative to using jumper wires such as these is soldering, which is more difficult and time-consuming! The "male to female" distinction indicates that one end has a male connector and the other end has a female connector.

Product link: www.alexwulff.com/radiobook/
links/jumpers ($6)

Battery Pack

We'll use a battery pack to power one of the transceivers used in Chapter 6. This allows you to move it around and observe how the signal changes! This battery pack requires six AA batteries—if you don't have any AA batteries, you will need to purchase these as well. The battery pack is shown in Figure 1-4.

Figure 1-4. *AA battery pack. Product link: www.alexwulff.com/ radiobook/links/batterypack ($7)*

Chapter 8: Handheld Transceivers and Repeaters

This is the first chapter in which you get to explore hardware related to amateur radio. Amateur radio can be a very equipment-intensive hobby, but there's inexpensive hardware that can do a lot.

Handheld Transceiver (HT)

This piece of hardware allows you to receive and transmit on amateur radio frequencies. Without the proper license, you are limited to receive functionality only; transmitting is against the law. We will go through the process of obtaining an amateur radio license later on in the book. This particular radio is extremely common due to its low cost and solid performance. This radio is enough to talk to amateur radio operators in your community or bounce messages off satellites to talk with individuals over a thousand miles away. This radio is shown in Figure 1-5.

Figure 1-5. *BaoFeng handheld transceiver. This BF-F8+ is almost identical to the UV-5R. Product link:* `www.alexwulff.com/radiobook/links/ht` *($30)*

Chapter 9: Amateur Radio Satellites

In this chapter, we utilize a special type of antenna to send and receive voice signals from satellites in space. This is a fun activity, but the antenna required is a significant investment. It is still possible to receive some signals from the antenna that comes with the handheld transceiver used in this book, but you will not be able to reach the satellite to talk with others. This advanced antenna can also be utilized for terrestrial communications. So you can opt to not purchase this antenna if you have budget constraints, but you will not be able to participate in some of the exercises in this chapter. If you don't purchase the antenna, you should still buy the BaoFeng programming cable.

Dualband Satellite Antenna

This is the directional (high-gain) antenna that we will later use to communicate with satellites. Rather than use the antenna in the mounted configuration shown in Figure 1-6, you'll hold it in your hand and follow a satellite across the sky with it as you communicate with the satellite. When ordering this antenna, make sure you select "UHF Connector" as the connector type at checkout.

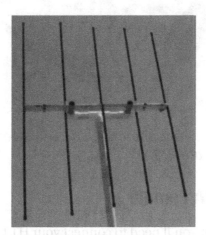

Figure 1-6. *2 m/70 cm-band five-element antenna. Image credit: Elk Antennas. Product link:* www.alexwulff.com/radiobook/links/sat-antenna *($130)*

BaoFeng Programming Cable

This cable (shown in Figure 1-7) enables you to upload channels from your computer to your radio. It is possible to program channels without it, but your life will be much easier with the cable! There are cheaper cables available online, but this is the only official one. Because it's official, it's very easy to find drivers for the cable, so I highly recommend purchasing this one.

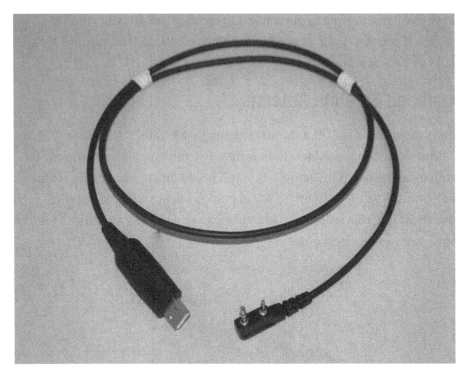

Figure 1-7. BaoFeng programming cable: www.alexwulff.com/
radiobook/links/cable ($20)

UHF Male to SMA Female

This is an adapter that you'll need to connect your HT to the log-periodic
antenna.

> Product link: www.alexwulff.com/radiobook/
> links/uhf-to-sma ($6)

SMA Cable

This cable will connect the adapter on the antenna to an adapter on your HT.

> Product link: www.alexwulff.com/radiobook/
> links/sma-cable ($6)

SMA Female to Female

This adapter is necessary to connect the SMA cable to your handheld transceiver.

Product link: www.alexwulff.com/radiobook/
links/sma-to-sma ($6)

Uses of Radio Communications Systems Today

Before actually learning about how radio communications systems work, it's important to identify their various uses in the modern world. Radio waves provide a few distinct advantages over other means of transmitting information, namely, their ability to propagate without the need for wires and the fact that they propagate information at the fastest possible speed. Additionally, radio waves are relatively easy to transmit and receive. Optical communications systems require more sophisticated hardware to encode and decode information in fiber-optic cables.

Wireless Device Connectivity

Communication for consumer electronics is one of the largest public-facing ways that radio communications systems impact the world. Many modern computing devices use electromagnetic radiation to send and receive the results of computations. A modern cell phone, such as the one in Figure 1-8, in addition to most tablets and computers, uses a combination of many different wireless communications standards to send and receive information.

Figure 1-8. *Modern iPhones use various radio bands and protocols to communicate with the outside world*

Cellular

Cellular networks, the namesake of cell phones, enable your smartphone to connect to the Internet and make and receive calls. Cell networks utilize immense amounts of communications infrastructure, such as the cell tower shown in Figure 1-9, to deliver packets of information to and from cell phones.

Figure 1-9. *A common cell tower*

All cell phones have external antenna bands that enable them to communicate with cell towers. Antennas, as will be discussed later, are a device's interface between electrical signals and electromagnetic radiation. A typical cell phone can connect with cell towers upward of a few miles away. Cell networks, or specifically the portion of the network that delivers data services, are a form of wide area network (WAN). Unsurprisingly, they get this designation as a result of covering a relatively large area with network coverage.

Wi-Fi

Wi-Fi is perhaps one of the most well-known communications protocols in existence. The word Wi-Fi is a trademark of the Wi-Fi alliance—its logo is shown in Figure 1-10.

13

Figure 1-10. *The official Wi-Fi logo*

Wi-Fi is actually a collection of wireless networking protocols, providing medium-range data services to and from a wired Ethernet connection. Wi-Fi is the fastest wireless communications protocol available for many consumer devices; it supports transmission of over 1 billion bits per second. Wi-Fi is a form of wireless local area network (WLAN). It does not get the designation of being a wide area network (WAN), as Wi-Fi is only designed to support a limited number of devices at a very limited range. Wi-Fi transmissions operate at a different frequency than those used for cellular, so Wi-Fi and cellular cannot share the same antenna on a device.

Bluetooth

Bluetooth is another well-known trademark describing a collection of wireless communications standards. Bluetooth is primarily used in connecting a central device such as a phone, tablet, or computer to a number of peripheral devices such as smartwatches, headphones, and other accessories. Bluetooth utilizes relatively little energy to transfer data, making it a popular choice for battery-powered devices. Due to its low power, Bluetooth can only operate across distances of a few tens of meters. This range limitation is why Bluetooth is designated as a personal area network (PAN). Bluetooth uses the same wireless frequencies as Wi-Fi, so the two oftentimes share an antenna.

GPS

GPS, as it is commonly used in conversation, is a colloquialism for any navigational device or system. However, GPS (short for Global Positioning System) actually refers to a specific satellite-based navigational system operated by the US government. GPS is a one-way communications system; GPS receivers do not send data back to the navigational satellites that make the system work. A GPS satellite is shown in Figure 1-11.

Figure 1-11. *A rendering of a GPS III satellite, produced by Lockheed Martin. The body of most GPS satellites is about the size of a small car and costs hundreds of millions of dollars to build and deploy.*

GPS receivers use the signals from a minimum of four satellites to pinpoint the device's current location. GPS satellites emit time signals, and the receiver uses the time difference between received signals to calculate its distance to each satellite. The GPS receiver then solves an algorithm that yields its coordinates. GPS is a service of the US military, which reserves the right to disrupt or disable GPS to protect national security. As such, many other countries have their own satellite-based navigational systems. Most GPS receivers also include support for these other navigational systems to improve accuracy.

Long-Distance Communications

While not as public-facing as communications networks for personal electronics, long-range radio links are crucial to the modern world. No other means of communication provides the data transfer rates, ease of operation, and mobility that radio affords for the most demanding of uses.

Marine Radio

Maritime radio communication is a very common example of a direct, long-distance radio link. Ships utilize predetermined frequencies, or channels, to communicate with one another. These channels lie in the VHF band of frequencies, which will be discussed later. The International Telecommunication Union (ITU) regulates channel allocation and use. Every large vessel—and practically every medium and small seafaring vessel—is equipped with a VHF antenna and radio designed to operate at marine frequencies. An example of such an antenna is shown in Figure 1-12.

Figure 1-12. *Practically every seafaring vessel is adorned with one or more antennas—the boat in this figure happens to have several*

Marine VHF radio is almost entirely voice based and can be used to communicate over distances no greater than 100 miles under normal conditions. Predefined channels exist for common tasks requiring communication, such as distress signals, port operations, ship-to-ship communications, and more. More sophisticated implementations of marine VHF radio support features such as text messaging and automatic ship identification.

Amateur Radio

Amateur radio will be discussed in great depth in subsequent chapters, but for now it's worth mentioning in the context of long-distance communications. Amateur radio can best be described as an international group of individuals interested in radio. Amateur radio operators, or hams, use specially allocated frequencies to communicate with one another. Such communications can be between individuals separated by everything from a few miles to a few continents, depending upon hardware configuration. An example of amateur radio hardware is shown in Figure 1-13.

Figure 1-13. *This handheld transceiver allows amateur radio operators to communicate across distances of a few miles*

Space-Based Communications

Objects in space have no better way to communicate with Earth than through radio communications. Transmitters and antennas on various spacecraft enable long-distance and high-throughput data links to Earth.

Satellite Data Services

For many locations away from population centers, a satellite link is the only possible means of communication with the outside world. Some satellite data services provide small, portable devices with a low-data-rate connection. Satellite phones and portable communications devices use such networks. Other satellite data networks provide large, fixed sites with a high-data-rate connection. Satellite Internet and TV rely on these types of systems. See Chapter 10 for a more in-depth description of these networks.

Deep-Space Communications

Radio is the only option for space missions to send data to Earth and receive communications from Earth. Most space missions are equipped with two types of communications systems: a highly directional antenna that supports long-distance communication but requires precise aiming (see Figure 1-14) and an omnidirectional but shorter-range system. Massive radio dishes on Earth receive the transmissions from various missions and relay the transmissions to mission operators.

Figure 1-14. *An artist's visualization of the Cassini-Huygens spacecraft approaching Saturn. Cassini-Huygens, designed to study Saturn and its moons, utilized a high-gain antenna to send science data back to Earth. This antenna, the large dish at the front of the spacecraft, is featured prominently in this figure*

Broadcasting

Considering that most people associate the word "radio" with music broadcasting, any list of modern uses of radio communications would be remiss without mentioning broadcasting. Radio broadcast systems are characterized by their one-way nature: a large transmitter sends a signal out over a large area, and a smaller receiver picks up this signal from many miles away. The word "broadcast" captures this sentiment perfectly.

AM and FM Radio

We will discuss AM and FM radio in greater depth in other parts of this book, but for now it's worth mentioning what they are and how they work. AM, or "amplitude modulation," and FM, or "frequency modulation," are two means of encoding information on top of a radio wave. AM and FM have become colloquially associated with music and voice broadcasts of a certain frequency band, but know that they are general techniques. "AM radio" or "FM radio" is used to specifically denote the music and voice broadcasts that you're likely familiar with.

AM radio and FM radio each use different frequency bands and have their own strengths and drawbacks: FM radio transmits a higher-bandwidth signal than AM radio, but cannot propagate as far as AM radio.

Broadcast Television

Broadcast television is one of the few applications of radio communications technology that has declined in usage in recent years. The frequency ranges allotted to broadcast television are huge and occupy a very useful place in the electromagnetic spectrum. Many governments have been repurposing these frequency allocations and are auctioning them off to telecommunications companies to deploy cellular networks on the frequencies.

Despite these changes, broadcast television signals are still common. Signals were originally broadcast in an analog format, but most countries have switched over to digital transmissions. Areas lacking in telecommunications infrastructure benefit from broadcast television's ability to provide television to far away and isolated locales. Many of the large antennas that you see on top of structures, such as the one in Figure 1-15, are or once were utilized to receive broadcast TV signals. Cable television has surpassed broadcast television in many places, as it offers more channels at a higher quality.

Figure 1-15. *A directional antenna mounted on top of a home for the purpose of receiving broadcast TV. We will discuss this specific type of antenna in Chapter 3*

Summary

This is by no means a comprehensive list of every use of radio communications. Rather, it is meant to show you the extent to which radio communication is integrated into the modern world. Throughout this text, you will learn the principles that enable all these applications of radio to be possible. Despite how different and complex each of the preceding systems may appear, they all rely on fundamental concepts such as propagation and modulation to transmit data. The beauty of radio communications stems from this concept: with one shared resource, the electromagnetic spectrum, myriad uses are possible.

In the next chapter, you will learn the basics of radio waves. Radio waves form the basis of any radio communications system, so understanding their behavior is crucial. You'll learn more about what exactly radio waves are, how they propagate, and how they interact with their environment.

CHAPTER 2

Basic Radio Theory

The purpose of this chapter is to give you a basic but intuitive understanding of what radio waves are and how radio waves propagate. We will walk through basics of the electromagnetic spectrum and properties of waves as they interact with matter.

The Electromagnetic Spectrum

Figure 2-1 is a common depiction of the electromagnetic spectrum. Many know the term "electromagnetic spectrum" or "electromagnetic radiation," but few can characterize exactly what these words signify. The electromagnetic spectrum encompasses all different types of electromagnetic radiation, all the way from the lowest-frequency radio waves to the highest-frequency gamma waves.

© Alex Wulff 2019
A. Wulff, *Beginning Radio Communications*,
https://doi.org/10.1007/978-1-4842-5302-1_2

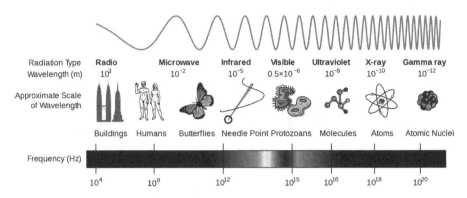

Figure 2-1. *The electromagnetic spectrum.*
Source: `http://mynasadata.larc.nasa.gov/images/EM_`
`Spectrum3-new.jpg`

Our entire existence depends upon electromagnetic radiation. Electromagnetic waves can travel through a vacuum, which allows the sun to heat our planet across vast expanses of empty space. Far-flung galaxies and stars emit electromagnetic waves which allow us to explore our universe. Our eyes detect electromagnetic radiation in the form of light that allows us to see. All of the world's economies, militaries, and technology industries are dependent upon electromagnetic waves to transmit information.

As mentioned, radio waves are just a small part of the larger electromagnetic spectrum. The property that makes them behave differently than another portion, such as visible light, is *wavelength/frequency*.

Note   Electromagnetic waves such as radio waves exhibit properties of both particles and waves, but for the purposes of this book, we will only consider and discuss the wave-like properties.

CHAPTER 2   BASIC RADIO THEORY

Wavelength and Frequency

I define wavelength, for the purposes of this book, as the distance between successive peaks in an electromagnetic wave. Wavelength governs many properties of how electromagnetic radiation interacts with its environment.

You may not be familiar with characterizing electromagnetic radiation by its wavelength, but you're certainly familiar with characterizing it by its *frequency*. Wavelength and frequency are inversely proportional; a wave's frequency is simply the speed of the wave divided by its wavelength.

All electromagnetic radiation propagates through free space (i.e., a vacuum) at the speed of light, or *c*. Therefore, the formula for wavelength for electromagnetic radiation is

$$\text{Wavelength} = c \,/\, \text{Frequency}$$

When you tune the FM radio in your car to 98.1 (or whatever your preferred station is), you're actually selecting what frequency of radio waves your car's audio system should utilize. In the case of FM, this frequency is on the scale of *megahertz*. Hertz is the SI unit of frequency; 1 Hz corresponds to one cycle per second. For an electromagnetic wave, a "cycle" would be an entire period of a wave passing by an observer. So peaks of electromagnetic waves in the range of FM radio pass by an observer millions of times per second.

Note If you're not familiar with metric prefixes such as mega, now would be the time to study these. This is something that we will utilize extensively throughout the rest of this book.

Radio Bands and Their Uses

The International Telecommunication Union, or ITU, designates 12 radio bands with the frequencies and wavelengths listed in Table 2-1. Characterizing radio waves as such is useful because frequencies inside each of these bands exhibit roughly the same physical properties.

Table 2-1. *A list of frequency ranges for radio waves and their associated characteristics*

Name	Frequency Range	Wavelength Range
ELF (Extremely Low Frequency)	3–30 Hz	100,000–10,000 km
SLF (Super Low Frequency)	30–300 Hz	10,000–1,000 km
ULF (Ultra Low Frequency)	300–3000 Hz	1,000–100 km
VLF (Very Low Frequency)	3–30 kHz	100–10 km
LF (Low Frequency)	30–300 kHz	10–1 km
MF (Medium Frequency)	300 kHz–3 MHz	1,000–100 m
HF (High Frequency)	3–30 MHz	100–10 m
VHF (Very High Frequency)	30 MHz–300 MHz	10–1 m
UHF (Ultra High Frequency)	300 MHz–3 GHz	1–0.1 m
SHF (Super High Frequency)	3 GHz–30 GHz	10–1 cm
EHF (Extremely High Frequency)	30–300 GHz	10–1 mm
THF (Tremendously High Frequency)	0.3 THz–30 THz	1–0.1 mm

ELF, SLF, ULF, and VLF

As we will explore later, lower-frequency waves cannot transmit information at a particularly high rate. This makes these bands only suitable for sending short, textual messages. An interesting property of this band is its incredible ability to penetrate the ground and ocean, as the ground and ocean normally block higher-frequency radio waves.

A practical use of this property is communication with submarines. Submarines normally have to come close to the surface in order to communicate with boats, satellites, and the mainland, but massive transmitters such as the one pictured in Figure 2-2 allow militaries to communicate with submerged submarines. This is a one-way link, as it is impractical to transmit ELF waves from a submarine. We will discuss transmitter characteristics such as this in the chapter on *antennas*.

Figure 2-2. *Clam Lake, Wisconsin, ELF submarine communications transmitter. Notice the long antenna running across the bottom-left of this image.*
Source: www.dodmedia.osd.mil/Assets/Still/1982/Navy/DN-SC-82-03911.JPEG

LF, MF, and HF

Radio waves with long wavelengths (such as in these bands) can exploit interesting effects of the Earth's atmosphere to travel extremely long distances. One can reflect waves in these bands off various layers in the atmosphere and ionosphere, making intercontinental communications possible. Figure 2-3 illustrates this property. These waves also can bend or diffract along the curvature of the Earth, making it possible to communicate over the horizon. We will discuss diffraction much more in the propagation section of this chapter.

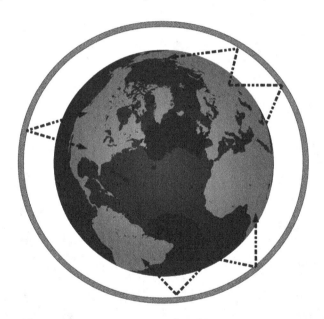

Figure 2-3. *Skywave propagation of radio waves.*
Source: https://en.wikipedia.org/wiki/Skywave#/media/
File:Skywave.jpg

Radio waves in these bands are capable of carrying low-quality voice signals, making these bands very popular for tasks such as maritime communications, some air traffic communications, and low-data tasks such as time signals for consumer clocks. AM radio also falls within this range.

VHF, UHF, and SHF

This section of the electromagnetic spectrum is considered the "beachfront property" of radio communications. Radio waves of these frequencies exhibit a good ability to transmit lots of information at relatively long distances. In these bands, you'll find most of the consumer radio technologies that you're already familiar with, such as FM radio, 3G/4G LTE, satellite radio, Wi-Fi, Bluetooth, and many more technologies. Figure 2-4 shows frequency allocations for this section of the electromagnetic spectrum; you're likely familiar with some of the technologies listed.

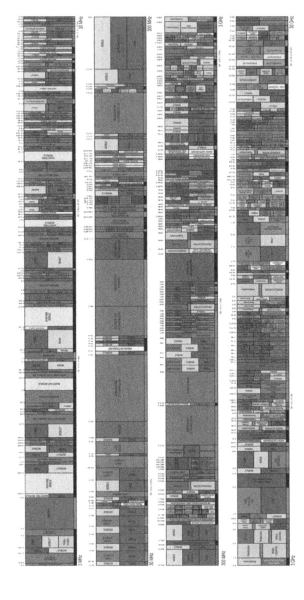

Figure 2-4. US frequency allocations from 3 MHz to 30 GHz. Full-size version available at www.ntia.doc.gov/files/ntia/publications/january_2016_spectrum_wall_chart.pdf

Due to the high value of certain bands within this range, governments actively regulate and police use of spectrum within their territories. Rights to very small slices of the spectrum, especially those used in cellular communications, can sell for billions of dollars at auction. In the United States, the Federal Communications Commission (FCC) levies millions of dollars in fines per year on individuals and corporations that operate unlicensed transmitters.

EHF

All radio waves within this band are classified as *microwaves*. The microwave range technically starts at around the UHF band, but different sources define microwaves in different ways. Microwaves are simply high-frequency radio waves; there's no real practical distinction between the two. Many systems, such as the space telescope in Figure 2-5, make use of microwave frequencies to carry out their missions.

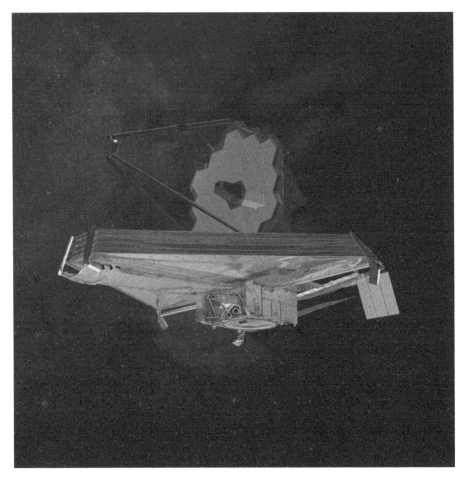

Figure 2-5. *An artist's rendering of the James Webb Space Telescope, which will utilize radio waves in the EHF range to send its science data back to Earth. Source: www.jwst.nasa.gov*

A useful feature of EHF-band communications is high data transfer rates. Space agencies around the globe utilize frequencies in this range to communicate with many satellites and science missions, and commercial communications satellites utilize this range for inter-satellite and satellite-ground communications. Point-to-point microwave links on Earth allow for companies to send large amounts of data across long distances.

Cellular communications are also expanding into frequency ranges in the EHF band. Many planned 5G systems rely on channels in the tens of gigahertz to deliver ultrafast cellular data links to mobile customers. Radar systems often operate using frequencies in the EHF range. These are used in everything from police speed detectors to missile guidance and tracking systems. Many frequencies within this band are readily absorbed by atmospheric gasses. Additionally, frequencies within this band are blocked by any obstacles in the path of the transmitter. As a result, a direct line of sight between the transmitter and receiver is often needed.

THF

THF radio waves occupy an "in-between space" of radio and light. The frequency of these waves is too high to easily generate and detect using digital and analog systems, but too low to be visible by humans or exhibit characteristics of light and even higher-frequency radiation. As such, research into radio waves has been primarily focused below THF. I am not aware of any practical communications systems that utilize THF waves to transmit information.

Propagation

Propagation is the way a wave travels through a medium. Electromagnetic waves have different propagation modes, with the type of mode generally depending upon wavelength and environmental characteristics. All the communication methods further discussed in this book propagate through the *line-of-sight* mode, although different propagation modes were mentioned in the section on LF, MF, and HF waves.

The term line of sight is somewhat misleading as it implies that a receiver must have a direct line of sight to the transmitter in order to get a signal. Obviously this is not the case for many wireless communications systems; one needn't see a router in order to have a Wi-Fi connection! A direct line-of-sight path is one in which the transmitter and receiver are visible to each other, such as in Figure 2-6. Direct line-of-sight paths are utilized in microwave data transmission links, among other things.

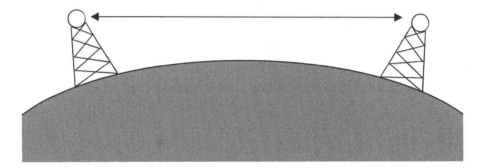

Figure 2-6. *Line-of-sight propagation between radio towers*

The general line-of-sight propagation mode can be more thought of as allowing one to communicate with something that one could see in the absence of any obstacles, that is, something not blocked by the curvature of the Earth or large geographic features like mountains.

The three general wave properties that govern line-of-sight propagation are *diffraction*, *reflection*, and *absorption*. I posit that through a good understanding of these properties, you can gain an intuitive understanding of radio propagation.

Diffraction

Diffraction is a general wave property that occurs when a wave meets a sharp transition. Upon meeting such a transition, the wave will spread out, or diffract, around the edge. In the context of radio communications, this means that a receiver shaded by some obstacle, such as a hill, can still receive signals from a distant transmitter. An example of diffraction is shown in Figure 2-7.

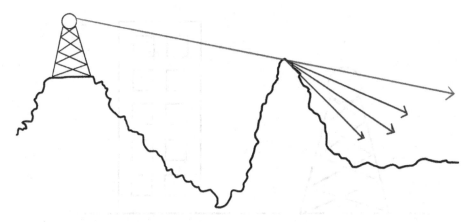

Figure 2-7. *Diffraction of radio waves around a geographic feature*

Diffraction occurs differently for waves with different frequencies. In general, lower-frequency waves are better at diffracting around large obstacles. Radio waves with a frequency lower than about 400 MHz, such as FM radio, can spread over a large geographic area because they can diffract around hills and buildings. Radio waves with a frequency higher than this are less effective at diffracting around geographic obstacles so are limited to shorter-range communications.

Diffraction is still extremely important in higher-frequency communications systems. The 2.4 GHz and 5 GHz radiation emitted from a Wi-Fi router diffracts around walls in houses to give you adequate coverage in your home (along with reflections, which we will discuss soon).

Reflection

Reflection is another general wave property that allows a receiver to communicate with an occluded transmitter. If a wave propagating through one medium reaches a different medium, the second medium will reflect back a portion of the wave's energy. Radio waves can reflect easily off of many large objects; Figure 2-8 illustrates this principle.

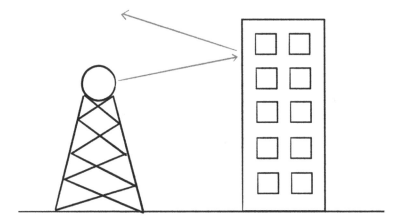

Figure 2-8. *Reflection of radio waves off a building*

These reflected waves can still carry useful information to a receiver. In urban environments, cell phone signals (usually in the range of 700 MHz–2 GHz) bounce off buildings as one way of reaching their target. Many wireless signals can take multiple reflected paths to a receiver. This is called *multipath* propagation, which can be both good and bad for wireless communications systems.

In general, good conductors (such as metal) reflect most of an electromagnetic wave's energy. Other materials like rock reflect some energy, and many insulators such as plastics reflect little energy. Areas covered in metal are well shielded from electromagnetic radiation, because the metal will reflect much of the incoming energy back.

Absorption

The energy not reflected by a medium will pass into the medium. Some materials allow electromagnetic radiation to pass through them without attenuation better than others. This is obviously another frequency-dependent phenomenon, as many materials do not allow visible light to pass at all but do pass lower-frequency radio waves. Radio waves can travel through most nonconductive materials, as illustrated in Figure 2-9.

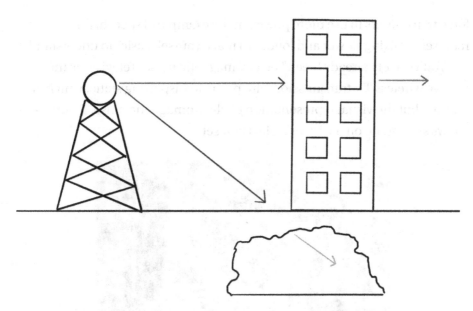

Figure 2-9. *Attenuation of radio waves by different features*

There's not much of a general trend for how much energy a material absorbs vs. how much it lets pass. The important things to understand here are general characteristics. Many signals pass somewhat well into aboveground structures, but are still slightly attenuated by them (try observing how your cell signal changes as you move outside). Other materials, such as thick concrete, block radio waves pretty well. In general, the ground will block most radio waves; this means that underground structures are well isolated against stray radio signals.

Noise

Noise is a concept that has an analog you already understand. In a noisy room, it can be difficult to hear something someone else says. This idea is no different for electromagnetic waves. Errant noise around the same frequency at which one is transmitting can vastly limit data transmission rates and force transmitters to use more power. In the example of speech, this represents talking slower and louder to make yourself easier to understand.

You've likely already "seen" electromagnetic noise. Televisions that receive wireless TV transmissions are prone to displaying static, which is nothing but the visual representation of electromagnetic noise. Figure 2-10 shows such static on a wireless television set.

Figure 2-10. *TV static is partially radio background noise*

Certain slices of the electromagnetic spectrum are extremely noisy, such as the unregulated 2.4 GHz band. Most of this noise is due to other devices transmitting in this frequency range. There is also a "noise floor" of background radiation that is always present.

The Doppler Effect

The *Doppler effect* is a general wave phenomenon that occurs with a moving transmitter or receiver (Figure 2-11). If a transmitter is moving at sufficient speed, electromagnetic waves will "bunch up" in front of the transmitter, making the waves appear at a higher frequency. Similarly, the waves will "spread out" behind the transmitter, making the waves appear at a lower frequency. Figure 2-11 provides a visual demonstration of this concept.

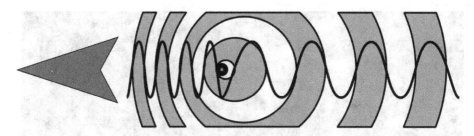

Figure 2-11. *The Doppler effect arising from a moving transmitter.*
Source: `https://commons.wikimedia.org/wiki/File:Doppler_`
`effect_diagrammatic.png`

Some radar systems use this effect to measure the velocity of objects; a radar gun can bounce radio waves of a set frequency off of cars and measure the returned frequency, allowing it to calculate the speed of the car.

We will directly observe this effect in some later examples on satellite communications. Satellites are fast-moving objects, and as we observe transmissions from some satellites, the transmit frequency will appear to shift as the satellite moves closer to us and then recedes.

An interesting corollary of the Doppler effect is the shifting of infrared, visible, and ultraviolet light from distant galaxies and other celestial objects. Many celestial objects move at a significant fraction of the speed of light relative to observers on Earth. As a result, light from these objects can appear shifted due to their motion. If an object is rapidly receding, its emissions will appear more reddish (or "redshifted"), and if an object is rapidly approaching, its emissions will appear more blueish (or "blueshifted"). Scientists can use this information to estimate the speed and range of distant celestial objects. A famous image from the Hubble Space Telescope, shown in Figure 2-12, captures this phenomenon.

Figure 2-12. *Hubble Ultra-Deep Field exhibiting red- and blueshifted galaxies*

An Aside on "Radiation"

Radio waves are classified as *nonionizing* radiation, which means that they lack the energy necessary to separate electrons from atoms. Ionizing electromagnetic radiation, such as ultraviolet light or x-rays, is energetic enough to cause adverse biological effects like DNA damage. On the other hand, the only known effect of radio waves on the human body is surface heating of tissue, which is completely harmless for all but the most powerful of transmitters. This is the principle that microwave ovens exploit to heat food.

The radio waves we interact with on a day-to-day basis pose little threat to human life. Scientists are still gathering information on the effects of long-term exposure to electromagnetic radiation such as that emitted by a cell phone, but for now there's no evidence to indicate that such exposure causes cancer or other adverse health effects. You may, however, encounter electromagnetic warning labels such as the one in Figure 2-13.

Figure 2-13. *A typical warning label applied to high-powered transmitters*

Such labels generally indicate the presence of a high-powered transmitter. Engineers do take precautions to limit exposure to electromagnetic radiation around these devices. Tissue heating can be dangerous, and the FCC sets limits on how much exposure to radio frequency (RF) radiation an individual should allow.

General Trends

In case you haven't already noticed, I described many of the preceding principles in a very broad manner. This is a recurring trend that you will see all throughout the domain of radio communications. A good communications engineer or electrical engineer has a comprehensive *intuitive* understanding of the concepts he or she uses. Having a general idea of what will happen in any given scenario is important, and this can be developed through practice and experimentation. There is a concrete mathematical basis for almost every phenomenon in radio communications, but very little of this is needed to understand the magic of radio.

So you can combine the preceding principles to generate an understanding of how radio waves will behave with *no* knowledge of the math and formulas behind them. In general, lower-frequency radiation propagates farther but can carry less information. This simple statement represents one of the fundamental trade-offs in radio communications systems. We will explore this throughout the rest of the text.

Summary

Radio waves are a fascinating phenomenon with broad impacts on our daily lives. As part of the electromagnetic spectrum, radio waves exhibit many of the same behaviors of light. Many of the differences in the behavior of radio waves as compared to light are a consequence of their relatively long wavelength (and thus low frequency). The difference in wavelength between different radio waves also leads to different properties among radio waves, which we classify through "bands."

In general, lower-frequency bands such as LF, MF, and HF can utilize special properties of radio waves and the Earth's atmosphere to travel long distances. These bands are not suitable for high data transfer rates, however. Bands of somewhat higher frequency, such as VHF and UHF, can still travel long distances but support high data transfer rates. This makes them very valuable for applications such as cellular data. The highest-frequency radio waves in the microwave region allow for extremely high data transfer rates, but oftentimes a direct line of sight between the transmitter and receiver is required.

Radio waves of the frequencies that we'll discuss in this book propagate through the line-of-sight propagation mode. Diffraction around sharp edges and reflections off obstacles allow transmitters and receivers without a direct line of sight to still communicate, although a direct line of sight will always yield the strongest signal.

In the next chapter, we will discuss antennas: the physics that govern their use, different types of antennas in use today, and how one can utilize an antenna for radio communications.

CHAPTER 3

Antennas

Antennas are the interface between the world of electronics and the world of electromagnetic radiation. All electronic devices depend on current, the flow of charge, and voltage, electric potential, to perform their intended function. An antenna can transform an alternating current (AC) into a radio wave and vice versa. In this chapter, we'll explore the physics that governs how antennas work and how you can use antennas to communicate. We'll cover everything from basic wire antennas to massive radio dishes such as those shown in Figure 3-1.

Figure 3-1. *Radio telescopes use parabolic antennas ("radio dishes") to detect radio waves from spacecraft and celestial objects*

© Alex Wulff 2019
A. Wulff, *Beginning Radio Communications*,
https://doi.org/10.1007/978-1-4842-5302-1_3

45

Electromagnetism

Electromagnetism is the field of study that encompasses charge, current, magnetism, and electric and magnetic fields. Electromagnetic waves are governed by the principles of electromagnetism; an electromagnetic wave is nothing but alternating electric and magnetic fields. You're already familiar with one type of electromagnetism: lightning. Lightning bolts, such as those shown in Figure 3-2, can produce intense electromagnetic waves.

Figure 3-2. *Lightning is a burst of current that produces very strong electromagnetic waves*

An alternating current within a conductor will produce an electromagnetic wave; antennas exploit this simple property to transmit information in the form of electromagnetic waves. Electric currents are very easy to produce and control, so antennas serve as an effective way to transmit and receive information without the use of a direct connection.

Electromagnetism provides the fundamental basis of all electromagnetic waves; but, thankfully for those learning about radio communications, very little knowledge of electromagnetism is required to understand how radio communication systems operate.

Current and Voltage

The "driving force" behind the electromagnetic waves emitted from an antenna is an electric current. Current is the flow of charge (electrons) per unit time, which is measured in amperes (A). The more charge flowing per second through a circuit, the higher the current. In general, the more current one can induce in an antenna, the stronger its emitted radiation, so almost all antennas are made from good conductors of current (metals).

In order to generate an electromagnetic wave from a conductor, one needs to apply an *alternating current* (AC). An alternating current is one in which the electrons move back and forth in a sinusoidal manner inside the conductor at a set frequency. Wall outlets supply alternating current to our devices at a frequency of 60 Hz, so there's a lot of 60 Hz noise that makes its way into radio systems from power lines and electrical wiring.

Another property of electromagnetism is electric potential, or voltage. Voltage is measured in units of volts (V). An applied potential in a circuit will coincide with a current. If there is no potential difference between two places in a circuit, then no current will flow between these two points. Charge always wants to move to areas of lower potential, and it takes energy to raise these electrons back to a higher potential. In many circuits, chemical reactions inside of a battery supply this energy to keep electrons flowing.

Current and voltage are related in an equation known as Ohm's law: $V = IR$, where V is voltage, I is current, and R is resistance. Therefore, for a given circuit, current and voltage are proportional.

Resistance is an intrinsic property of an object that depends on its geometry and material. The resistance of an object is a measure of how much it impedes the flow of electrons. Resistance is measured in ohms (Ω). Metal wires have very low resistances, on the order of 0.1 Ω per meter of wire, whereas insulators such as plastics have resistances many orders of magnitude greater than that.

For the purposes of this book, you can think of a voltage applied across a conductor as causing a current in that conductor, although in actuality the underlying mechanisms of electromagnetism tell a slightly different story. Wall outlets in the United States supply a potential of 120 V to electronic devices in our homes. Many devices have circuitry that lowers this voltage and converts the resulting current into *direct current* (DC), which is a linear flow of charge without any oscillation. Direct current flowing through a conductor does not produce electromagnetic radiation, but it is useful in sensitive digital equipment such as smartphones and computers which operate entirely using DC. In fact, one of the only uses of alternating current in such circuits is for radio systems.

Power

Power is a measure of energy per unit of time. In the context of antennas, the power dissipated by an antenna shows how much energy this antenna radiates per unit of time. Power is measured in watts (W) and is given by $P = IV$ (power is current times voltage), or $P = I^2R$ (the current squared times the resistance of a material) for resistive loads. The amount of energy you utilize in your home is often measured in kilowatt hours (kWh). If a home consumes 1000 kWh in a month, one could expend the same amount of energy by consuming 1000 kW (1 MW) of power over the span of 1 hour or, equivalently, 1 kW for 1000 hours.

Communications and electrical engineers often measure the energy output of antennas in terms of watts. Table 3-1 gives the output or input energy of various systems.

Table 3-1. *A list of various electronic systems and their associated output power*

System	Typical Power
Wi-Fi router	100 mW
Cell phone antenna	3 W
Voyager spacecraft transmitter	~20 W
Geostationary communications satellite antenna	~100 W
FM radio station antenna	1 kW
AM radio station antenna	50 kW
Most powerful AM radio stations' antennas	2 MW
Power output of a nuclear power plant	1000 MW

The Voyager spacecraft are a fascinating case. Using around 20 W, Voyager 1 is able to communicate with Earth over a distance of more than 13 billion miles. Estimates place the power received on Earth from this spacecraft at around 10^{-16} W, which is only detectable by extremely large radio dishes and is barely above the power of ambient radio noise. NASA utilizes a network of global network of these dishes, such as those shown in Figure 3-3, to receive this puny signal.

Figure 3-3. *Radio dishes used to communicate with the Voyager spacecraft as a part of the Deep Space Network*

Resonance

A given antenna can be utilized to transmit across many different frequencies, but antennas are always most effective around their resonant frequencies. For an antenna receiving radiation, incoming radiation of the resonant frequency helps magnify currents inside the antenna from previous radiation, creating a compounding effect. Other frequencies can be particularly ineffective at inducing current in an antenna because incoming radiation can actually create currents that oppose existing current. This same principle occurs in reverse for transmitting.

The resonant frequencies of an antenna are mostly determined by its length. Many antennas resonate at odd multiples of ¼-wavelength. This means that if a quarter of a given frequency's wavelength is some odd multiple of the length of the antenna, the antenna will likely resonate at that frequency. Let's take 144 MHz waves as an example. The wavelength is 300,000,000 m/s / 144,000,000 Hz ≈ 2 m, so a resonant receiving antenna would be approximately 50 cm (or odd multiples thereof).

Antenna Properties

Similar to radio propagation, there are a number of properties of antennas that govern their use. Through an understanding of these properties, you can gain an intuitive understanding of how an antenna will operate without knowing much about electromagnetism. The properties that we will explore are

- *Gain*

- *Radiation pattern*

- *Bandwidth*

- *Polarization*

Gain

The *gain* of an antenna refers to how much energy an antenna radiates in a particular direction. Antennas do not radiate energy equally in all directions, which is a useful property that one can exploit to make highly directional antennas. Gain in the general sense of the term is nothing but the ratio between the output and input power of a system. As such, the gain of a system must always refer to some baseline. In the case of antennas, this baseline is a theoretical antenna called an *isotropic antenna* (see Figure 3-4).

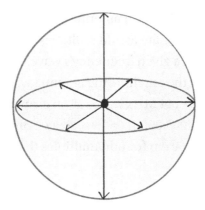

Figure 3-4. *A drawing of an isotropic antenna. The antenna is the dot at the center, and its radiation pattern is drawn*

An isotropic antenna radiates any input energy equally in all directions. This is impossible to construct in practice, although there are types of antennas that have similar characteristics. The gain of an antenna in any given direction is the ratio between the radiated power in that direction and the expected radiated power from an isotropic antenna. This is known as *isotropic gain.*

Isotropic gain can be expressed as the raw ratio, but it is more often measured in units of *decibels-isotropic,* or dBi. The decibel scale is used extensively to characterize the gain of many systems in scientific and engineering contexts. The decibel scale is always logarithmic, meaning that a doubling of output to input ratio results in a linear increase in gain. The definition of isotropic gain is

$$G_{dBi} = 10 \cdot \log_{10}\left(G_{ratio}\right)$$

A doubling of power with respect to an isotropic antenna yields a gain increase of approximately 3 dBi. You can easily show this through the gain formula: $10 \cdot \log_{10}(1) = 0$ (a ratio of 1 corresponds to zero gain), $10 \cdot \log_{10}(2) = 3.01$, $10 \cdot \log_{10}(4) = 6.02$, and so on.

An antenna will only have a fixed amount of input power to radiate; if the radiated power of an antenna is greater in a particular direction than an isotropic antenna with the same input power, then the radiated power must be less than that of an isotropic antenna in another direction. Antennas are *passive* elements, meaning that they do not contribute any energy to a system; antennas merely transform electromagnetic waves into current and vice versa. There will always be this trade-off between more radiated power in one direction and less in others for any type of antenna.

Antenna gain is symmetric for transmitting and receiving. If an antenna radiates more power in a particular direction, then this antenna will also be better at receiving electromagnetic waves in that particular direction.

Beam/Radiation Patterns

One can represent the gain of an antenna in all directions through a plot of its radiation pattern. The radiation pattern of an antenna is nothing but a 3D or 2D plot of an antenna's isotropic gain as measured from an observer a fair distance away. An antenna can be constructed in a computer-aided design (CAD) program that will then simulate this antenna's radiation pattern. The radiation pattern of antennas can be physically measured by moving a highly calibrated receive antenna around the transmitting antenna to capture its gain at specific points.

We will now discuss basic types of antennas, their merits, and their radiation patterns. I have modelled all these antennas in one of the aforementioned CAD programs and included images of the calculated radiation patterns. The gain of most of these images is measured in dBi; when represented in ratio form, many of the nuanced features of the radiation patterns disappear, as logarithmic scales tend to accentuate smaller features and make more powerful features less prominent.

Dipole

A dipole antenna is one of the most widely used antenna types. It is oftentimes used on its own to transmit and receive radio waves, or it can be a part of a larger antenna structure containing multiple elements. As shown in the radiation pattern, dipoles radiate most of their energy along their length. They exhibit a *null,* or area of low radiation, around the top of the antenna. See Figures 3-5 and 3-6 for the appearance of a typical dipole antenna and a simulation of its radiation pattern.

Figure 3-5. *A model of a dipole, which is just a wire with the feed (red dot) in the middle*

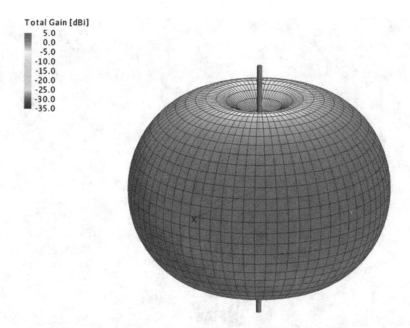

Figure 3-6. *Dipole antenna's radiation pattern in dBi*

Dipoles are usually comprised of two colinear quarter-wavelength elements that are connected to the source. Since the total length of the antenna is half a wavelength, this particular variety is called a *half-wave* dipole. A very common use of dipole antennas is in cellular communications. Most cell towers look similar to the one in Figure 3-7.

Figure 3-7. *A standard cellular communications tower with sector antennas*

The rectangular-looking objects on the cell tower are called *sector antennas*, which are nothing but a few dipoles stacked vertically. A metallic surface behind the dipoles reflects their energy outward to cover roughly 120 degrees in azimuth around the tower.

Monopole/Whip

Monopole antennas are similar to dipole antennas in their radiation pattern and their operation. The difference is that monopole antennas generally have their feed point at the bottom of the segment of wire, and the total antenna length is generally one quarter-wavelength. As shown in Figures 3-8 and 3-9, there are many similarities between the monopole and dipole antenna types.

Figure 3-8. *A monopole antenna model; note the red feed point at the bottom as opposed to the middle with the dipole*

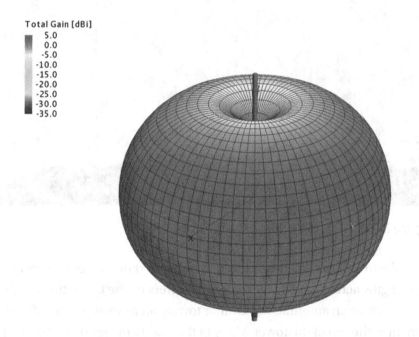

Figure 3-9. *The radiation pattern of a monopole antenna; it is very similar to that of a dipole*

Monopole antennas only have one length of wire that radiates energy, hence why they're called "monopole" antennas as opposed to dipole antennas which have two lengths of wire that radiate. One can commonly see monopole antennas in the form of *mast radiators*, or radio towers as they are colloquially known. Figure 3-10 shows a collection of mast radiators.

Figure 3-10. *A variety of mast radiators*

Radio towers are often employed to transmit radio waves with long wavelengths across long distances. Some towers utilize the entire length of the tower as an antenna, while other towers merely support a radiating element at the top of the tower. Many of the towers in Figure 3-10 support a large monopole antenna at the top of the tower.

Yagi

Yagi antennas employ a variety of *driven* and *parasitic* elements to create a highly directional beam. The longest and farthest back element is a reflector, which gives the antenna forward directionality. Next is the driven element, which is a dipole antenna connected to the source. Subsequent elements are not connected to the source, just like the reflector; their job is to absorb and reradiate the energy emitted from the dipole to give the antenna further directionality (this is why they're known as parasitic elements). Figures 3-11, 3-12, and 3-13 show the appearance and radiation pattern of a Yagi antenna.

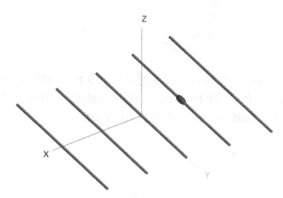

Figure 3-11. *An isometric view of a model of a Yagi antenna. The radiating element is the second from the right. Most elements are slightly different lengths*

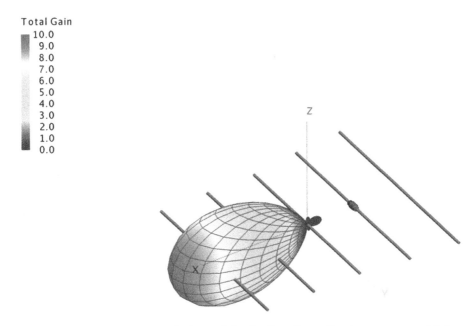

Figure 3-12. *A gain-scaled model of a Yagi's radiation pattern. Take no note of the fact that the radiation emanates from the element in the middle; this point was merely chosen to be the origin*

Total Gain [dBi]
10.0
5.0
0.0
-5.0
-10.0
-15.0
-20.0
-25.0
-30.0

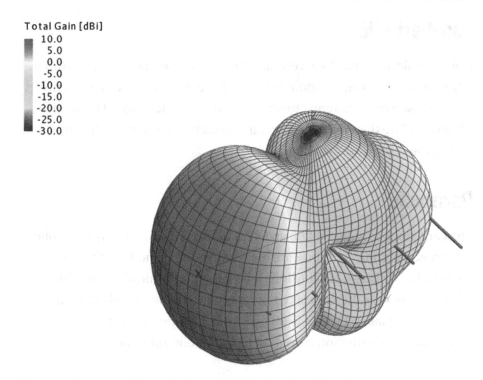

Figure 3-13. *A dBi-scaled model of a Yagi's radiation pattern*

One can commonly see Yagi antennas on the roofs of buildings. Back when most television was still transmitted over the air, many homes used directional Yagis to achieve good reception. One item to note in the radiation patterns pictured above is the difference between the raw gain-scaled image and the image that is scaled in dBi. Logarithmic scales accentuate features of lower magnitude, so it's possible to see minute details of the radiation pattern that disappear on the gain-scaled image. In actuality, these features are hundreds of times lower magnitude than the main beam pictured in the gain-scaled image.

61

Log-Periodic

Log-periodic antennas look very similar to Yagi antennas but operate in a different manner. Log-periodic antennas have multiple driven elements which allow a given antenna to operate across a wide range of frequencies. We will explore this concept further in the section on *bandwidth*. Log-periodic antennas are also directional.

Parabolic

Most antennas commonly known as "radio dishes" are actually parabolic antennas. Parabolic antennas are highly directional and help the operator collect a lot of energy, making long-distance communications feasible. These are perhaps the easiest type of antenna to identify and are seen in numerous places. Figures 3-14, 3-15, and 3-16 demonstrate the appearance and radiation pattern of the parabolic antenna.

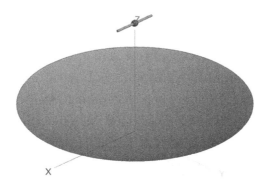

Figure 3-14. A simple parabolic antenna comprised of a dipole and a parabolic reflector

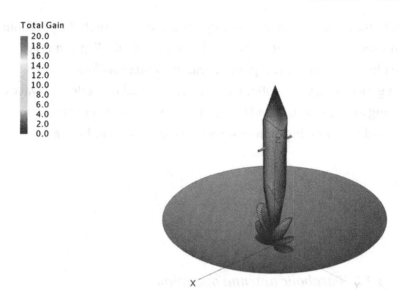

Figure 3-15. *A gain-scaled image of this parabolic antenna's radiation pattern*

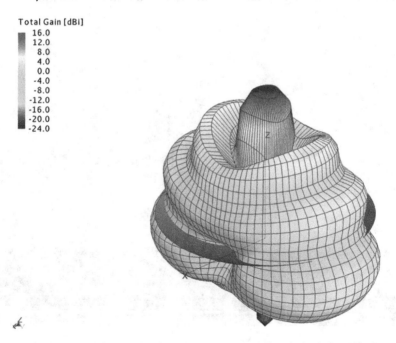

Figure 3-16. *A dBi-scaled image of this parabolic antenna's radiation pattern*

Parabolic antennas are commonly comprised of a metallic parabolic dish and some feed element offset in the center of this dish at a very precise place called the focal point. Parabolic antennas function by reflecting incoming waves off the dish once, with all the reflected waves combining at one point, called the *focal point*. This concept is easy to understand after looking at how such a dish functions in Figure 3-17.

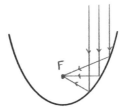

Figure 3-17. *Parabolic antenna operation*

Many cell towers with sector antennas, such as the one in Figure 3-18, also have drum-looking structures mounted in a different location.

Figure 3-18. *A cellular communications tower with parabolic antennas covered by a radome*

These objects are actually parabolic antennas covered by a *radome*. Radomes are radio-transparent devices (radio waves pass through them unhindered) that protect the parabolic antennas from the weather. These parabolic antennas provide high-capacity data links to and from the tower that allow it to communicate with other towers and stations on the ground. This minimizes the amount of wiring and infrastructure necessary to deploy new towers. Such links are highly directional and oftentimes require a direct line of sight between other dishes.

Another common application of parabolic antennas is in radio astronomy and satellite communications. Since radio antennas are highly directional and have the capability of collecting lots of energy from a distant receiver, they are well suited to this use case. The only downside of such antennas is that they must be pointed directly at their target to be effective. A difference of only a few degrees can cause stations on Earth to lose communications with a spacecraft; such a spacecraft is shown in Figure 3-19.

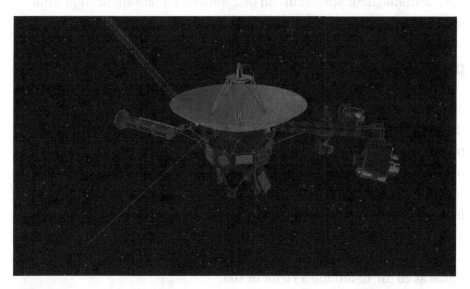

Figure 3-19. *Spacecraft such as Voyager (pictured here) employ high-gain parabolic antennas to communicate with distant targets. Voyager's parabolic antenna is the large dish at the center of the spacecraft*

Bandwidth

Due to the principles of resonance that we discussed above, many antennas can only transmit and receive across narrow bands of frequency. A way to express this quality of a given antenna is *bandwidth*. Bandwidth is a measure of how good an antenna is at radiating energy across a varied frequency range. Some antennas have a very narrow bandwidth, while others can transmit across large frequency ranges.

A narrow bandwidth can be both good and bad depending upon the application. If one wants to transmit or receive information at many different frequencies, a narrow bandwidth is undesirable. Alternatively, a narrow bandwidth can be a useful property to filter out noise from adjacent parts of the spectrum for receiving. This idea of fundamental trade-offs is a recurring theme throughout the realm of radio communications; many properties of communications equipment and the electromagnetic spectrum can be exploited for one application while introducing complexities for another application.

Polarization

Most antennas emit *polarized radiation*, or electromagnetic radiation that is directionally oriented. In the context of antennas, the concept of polarization requires that transmitting and receiving antennas must be oriented in the same direction in order to function properly. Dipole and monopole antennas are polarized, which means that antennas derived from monopoles and dipoles, such as some parabolic antennas and Yagis, are also polarized. A 90-degree difference between the transmitting antenna and the receiving antenna can attenuate the received signal by as much as 20 dB, or around a factor of 100.

Summary

The physics that governs antennas, and radio waves in general, lies primarily in the domain of electromagnetism. Radio waves are nothing but alternating electric and magnetic fields. The length of an antenna is a function of the wavelength of radio wave it's designed to emit. As shown by the radiation patterns in this chapter, one can arrange basic antenna types in creative ways to serve a variety of tasks. The monopole and dipole antennas form the building blocks of the more complex antennas, such as the directional Yagi and parabolic antennas.

Hopefully, antennas are now not just some strange device you see on the side of homes or on top of large poles; antennas are the backbone of many communications networks, so understanding various antenna properties is crucial to gaining a complete picture of radio communications. There is still so much to learn about antennas. This chapter glossed over many of the details of how antennas actually radiate, the role phase plays in these systems, and many other points; so, if your interest has been piqued, I highly recommend doing more of your own research.

Much like with radio wave propagation, it's not necessarily important to have a concrete mathematical basis of how antennas operate. Rather, make sure you understand the basic principles and antenna types discussed in this chapter, and you'll be well on your way to becoming proficient in radio communications. In the next chapter, you'll get to take your first dive into radio communications by downloading information from National Oceanic and Atmospheric Administration (NOAA) weather satellites via radio waves.

CHAPTER 4

Project: Satellite Imagery

In this chapter, we'll use a software-defined radio to receive image data from NOAA weather satellites flying overhead and then render this data into a real image. Your newfound knowledge of radio theory will be plenty sufficient for you to understand what's happening behind the scenes. You'll need a laptop for this chapter, or a desktop very close to a window, as actually capturing data from the satellites must be done outside. Figure 4-1 shows what the final image from a satellite will look like.

Figure 4-1. *A real image pulled from NOAA weather satellites; yours will look similar!*

© Alex Wulff 2019
A. Wulff, *Beginning Radio Communications*,
https://doi.org/10.1007/978-1-4842-5302-1_4

Software-Defined Radio

Software-defined radios, or SDRs, are devices that allow computers to receive raw electromagnetic information at a programmable frequency. In their simplest form, software-defined radios take in the frequency and bandwidth the user wishes to sample, along with a sampling rate, and return to the user values from the antenna at that given frequency at the sampling rate specified. Figure 4-2 shows the software-defined radio used in this chapter.

Figure 4-2. *The software-defined radio that we use in this text*

A circuit inside of the software-defined radio is tunable such that only energy at the desired frequency is sampled; the rest of the electromagnetic spectrum exciting the antenna is ignored. Since this system is in fact tunable, one must also adjust the antenna length for maximum performance. The software-defined radio kit mentioned at the beginning of this book, which utilizes a device known as "RTL-SDR," comes with a telescoping antenna, so the user can adjust its length for different frequencies. The RTL-SDR device is capable of receiving frequencies of around 20 MHz–2 GHz.

In summary, software-defined radios are computer-tunable devices that allow one to listen to a large swath of the electromagnetic spectrum.

The Satellites

Out of the tens of thousands of satellites whizzing by or remaining stationary overhead, we will try and receive communications from just three. These three satellites are NOAA-15, NOAA-18, and NOAA-19. NOAA 18 is shown in Figure 4-3.

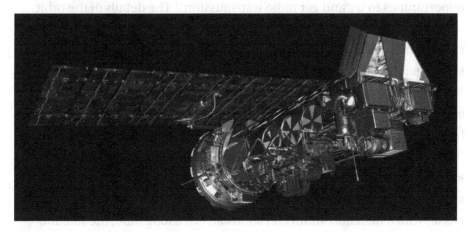

Figure 4-3. *NOAA-18, one of the satellites from which we'll gather data*

NOAA, or the National Oceanic and Atmospheric Administration (of the United States), operates a fleet of satellites primarily for climate and meteorological monitoring. These satellites are equipped with a wide variety of sensors, but only the image data transmitted from the satellites is of interest to us. The three satellites mentioned above transmit images at a frequency that's easy to receive and in a format that's easy to decode.

These satellites move around the Earth in a configuration known as a *sun-synchronous orbit.* The mathematical details of such an orbit are out of the purview of this text, but the physical orbits themselves are not too difficult to understand. These satellites orbit roughly north to south (or south to north depending on where the satellite is) and move sideways across the globe roughly 1000 miles with each orbit. They are also at a height such that they can see a patch of the Earth roughly 3000 miles in diameter. The satellites take around 100 minutes to complete one orbit of the Earth.

The configurations of the orbits, and the fact that there are three satellites, mean that one should be visible in the sky (and thus able to receive transmissions from) every few hours. This will give you plenty of opportunities to try and get radio transmissions! The details of the orbit work out such that one of these NOAA satellites will take 10–20 minutes to cross your sky. If the satellite passes directly overhead, it will appear in the sky longer than if it were to pass by closer to the horizon.

Satellite passes such as these are characterized by their maximum elevation, or the maximum angle the satellite makes between it and a horizontal plane. This is roughly equivalent to the maximum angle between the satellite and the horizon. A satellite with a low maximum elevation will appear very low in the sky, the duration of the pass will be short, and the satellite will stay close to one cardinal direction during the pass. In contrast, passes with a high maximum elevation can last a long time; the satellite will fly almost directly overhead and will come above the horizon in one direction and go back below the horizon in the opposite direction.
A diagram of an orbit is shown in Figure 4-4.

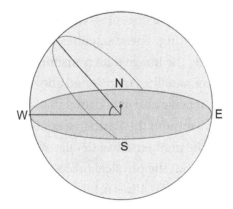

Figure 4-4. *A diagram illustrating the path of a satellite across the sky*

The middle plane in the figure represents the ground—everything above this is visible sky. The arc is the path of an orbiting object across the sky. This pass has a maximum elevation of roughly 40 degrees.

For this application, passes with a higher elevation are better for a number of reasons. Firstly, a longer duration means the received picture will be larger. These satellites transmit images of the ground as they pass by, so the longer you receive transmissions from the satellite, the more of the ground you will be able to see. Secondly, the quality of the signal will be much better for higher-elevation passes. When the satellite is higher in the sky, there's less of a chance of its signal being attenuated by trees and buildings. Additionally, the satellite is closest to you when it's directly overhead, so the received signal will be the strongest.

Initial Antenna Setup

Before messing around with any software, you'll need to set up the SDR's antenna first. To do this, first screw the two longer telescoping antennas into the antenna mount included with the kit. Attach one end of the long cable included in the kit to the output of the antenna mount, and then screw the other end into the exposed connector on the RTL-SDR device. Expand the antennas, and you're good to go! Put this aside for now—we'll use it later to verify that the software is working.

Necessary Software

Now that we've gotten the theory and antenna preparation out of the way, you can begin to set up the software necessary to receive and decode satellite images! There are three basic programs necessary, which are listed in the following. I set up this workflow in macOS, but I will detail how to do this in both macOS and Windows. Screenshots are in macOS, so Windows interfaces may look slightly different.

- **SDR Software:** We'll need a program to control the software-defined radio and output the received audio. Programs of this type configure the SDR, take in the raw data, decode it, and output information as audio. More advanced programs can perform more complex decoding, but for this application, we only require a program that can decode frequency-modulated audio (more on this later).

- **Audio-to-Image Software:** These NOAA satellites utilize an analog picture transmission (abbreviated APT) format. The SDR program outputs audio that gets turned into a real image by this program.

- **Audio Piping Software:** We'll need a link between the SDR program and the audio-to-image software. Basic audio piping programs imitate output devices like speakers for one program and input devices like microphones for other programs. This allows us to send audio from one program to another in a seamless manner.

SDR Software: CubicSDR

The program that we will use to control the RTL-SDR device is CubicSDR. All SDR programs contain the same basic features:

- A waterfall plot that allows you to view the intensity of the electromagnetic spectrum across a section of frequencies

- A means of configuring the receive frequency and bandwidth of the radio

- A means of decoding the received information and outputting it in a certain format

CubicSDR's main interface window is shown in Figure 4-5. FM radio stations in my area are shown. The station farthest to the right transmits digital audio (branded "HD Radio") above and below the main analog signal, which is why it has those two strips on the side.

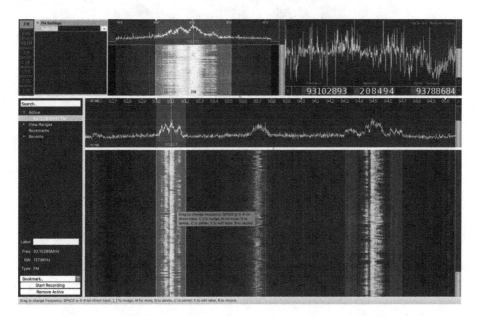

Figure 4-5. *CubicSDR's main interface*

CubicSDR checks all these boxes in addition to being free, cross-platform, and well designed. Start by downloading CubicSDR from https://github.com/cjcliffe/CubicSDR/releases. You can find the build for your platform in the "Assets" section. Choose the proper version, and install the software on your computer. The download will be a .dmg for macOS and a .exe for Windows.

If you're on Windows, you will need to follow the setup instructions at www.rtl-sdr.com/rtl-sdr-quick-start-guide/ to install the proper RTL-SDR drivers. Scroll down until you see instructions for using RTL-SDR with CubicSDR. If you're on a Mac, your device should work out of the box.

Plug your SDR into a free USB port, and start CubicSDR. You should plug the device in before starting CubicSDR. If all goes well, a window such as the one shown in Figure 4-6 should appear.

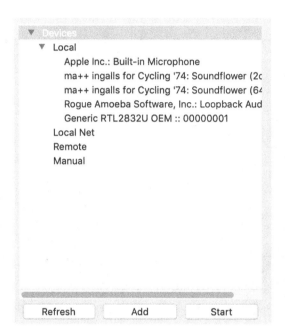

Figure 4-6. CubicSDR's startup window with my RTL-SDR device listed at the bottom

Upon startup, you should see an image similar to the one above. Select your SDR by clicking it—it will likely be labelled something like "Generic RTL ..." if you're using a Mac—and click "Start." The main interface will then appear. The various portions of the interface are labelled in Figure 4-7.

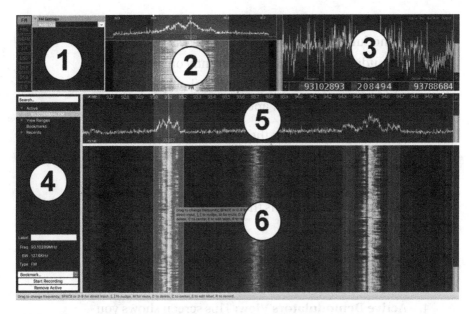

Figure 4-7. *CubicSDR's interface with labels*

This is CubicSDR's main interface. The term "demodulator" is used throughout the interface—a demodulator is simply a region of the electromagnetic spectrum that CubicSDR samples and converts to audio. You can enable a demodulator by clicking region **6**. The white-shaded area represents the bandwidth; CubicSDR will take all the received energy from this region and pass it through various demodulation filters. More will be said on modulation and demodulation later.

1. **Demodulator and Output Selection:** Here you can select the demodulator type (leave this on FM for now) and the output channel of the audio.

2. **Magnified Waterfall Plot:** When CubicSDR is actively demodulating a signal, a zoomed-in window of the main waterfall plot will appear here.

3. **Audio Output:** This is the result of the
   demodulation process; it shows the waveform of
   the audio that CubicSDR is currently outputting.
   This region also contains numerical outputs of the
   frequency, bandwidth, and *center frequency.*

   - *Frequency:* This is the center frequency of the
     active demodulator. This value will be blank until
     you add a demodulator.

   - *Bandwidth:* This is the bandwidth of the
     demodulator.

   - *Center Frequency:* This is the center frequency of
     the large waterfall plot.

4. **Active Demodulators View:** This screen shows you
   all the active demodulators and their frequencies.

5. **Instantaneous View:** This region is an
   instantaneous view of a slice of the electromagnetic
   spectrum. Frequency is on the X-axis, and power
   (scaled logarithmically) is on the Y-axis.

6. **Waterfall Plot:** This is the main waterfall plot
   showing the received power across a slice of the
   electromagnetic spectrum over time.

You can change the demodulation frequency, bandwidth, and center
frequency of the window using the numbers in region **3**. Moving your
mouse over the numbers will reveal arrows to change them, but after
changing a selection using the arrows, you can press the space key to enable
keyboard input. You can enter a value like 144 MHz by typing "144 M" and
pressing the enter key. Now that you're familiar with the interface, let's try
and actually receive something interesting!

1. Set the center frequency to 100 MHz, and you should see various bands of activity somewhere on the waterfall plot. These patches of activity are FM radio stations that transmit near 100 MHz.

2. Click the center of one with your mouse, and drag the edge of the white-shaded region to enclose all of the greenish signal.

3. Ensure that the output device in the top-left of your screen is set to the speakers on your computer, turn your volume up, and you should hear the radio station coming out of your computer!

4. The preceding figure (labelled with numbers) shows what CubicSDR's interface should look like after these steps.

Decoding Software: WXtoImg

WXtoImg is a rather archaic program that takes in audio from the NOAA satellites and converts it to an image. The software is no longer maintained, but a dedicated fan uploaded the last builds of WXtoImg to https://wxtoimgrestored.xyz. Navigate to this web site's downloads page, and download the correct version of the software for your system. Open it up, and you should be presented with a mostly gray screen with a few tabs. An example of this is shown in Figure 4-8.

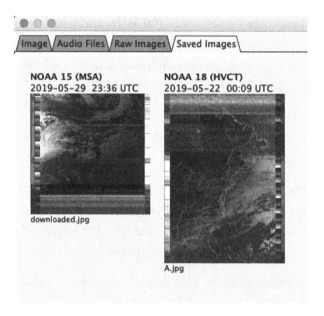

Figure 4-8. WXtoImg's interface window

Before you're ready to decode an image, you'll need to configure a few things first:

1. Go to the "Options" menu bar and select "Ground Station Location." Enter your latitude and longitude, and select "Ok."

2. Next, go to "File" and then "Update Keplers." This selection downloads tracking information for the three NOAA satellites of interest so the program knows when they'll fly overhead.

3. After this operation completes, you can select "Satellite Pass List" in the file menu, and WXtoImg will output a list of all the times the satellites will pass overhead. The important item here is "MEL," or maximum elevation. If the maximum elevation is too low, you'll get a very small and poor-quality

image—only passes with elevations of around 30 degrees or more will produce good results. You can still practice on lower-elevation passes. WXtoImg even gives you the frequency at which each of the satellites transmits (measured in MHz).

Piping Program

You now have an SDR program and a decoding program, but you need a way to link these two together. This is where the audio piping program comes in: it takes audio from CubicSDR and outputs it to WXtoImg. Audio piping programs imitate speakers for a program outputting sound and microphones for a program that takes sound as an input. Soundflower for macOS is my favorite; you can download it here: `https://github.com/mattingalls/Soundflower`. For Windows, VB-Cable (`www.vb-audio.com/Cable/`) is a good, free option. Download the program of your choice, and install it.

First Test

Testing your setup is important to ensuring the success of your first flyover. A good way to test everything is to pipe some random audio from CubicSDR to WXtoImg and have WXtoImg try and decode it. The image won't look pretty, but it will demonstrate that everything is functional.

1. Repeat the same steps you used to make CubicSDR output sound from a local FM station.

2. In the upper-left corner of CubicSDR, change the output device from your computer's speakers to the audio piping program. If everything was configured correctly, your audio piping program should appear as an output device in the list. This is shown in Figure 4-9.

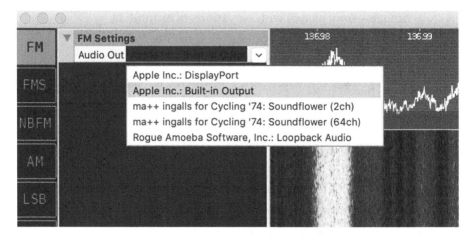

Figure 4-9. *A list of CubicSDR's possible output devices. In the case of macOS, one would select Soundflower (2ch) to pipe into Soundflower*

3. Now, open up WXtoImg and select "Recording Options" in the "Options" menu.

4. Under "Common recording options," select the dropdown next to "soundcard" and select your audio piping program.

5. Close this window by clicking "Ok," and then go to "Record" in the "File" menu. Make sure "Record and auto process" is selected, and finally click "Manual Test."

6. If all goes well, static such as that shown in Figure 4-10 should start to fill the screen line by line.

Figure 4-10. *FM radio audio "decoded" by WXtoImg. The red lines through the image are for the map overlay, with WXtoImg adds after the image is finished being decoded.*

WXtoImg processes the images from the satellites line by line, so you get to watch the image slowly appear during a real flyover. For now, WXtoImg is trying to decode the music coming from the FM station and turn it into an image. This music or voice won't translate to an image, which is why static appears. If the image is black, this indicates that WXtoImg isn't receiving any sound information. Try reconfiguring your audio piping program and checking that it is the output of CubicSDR and the input to WXtoImg using the mentioned dropdowns menus in both.

Antenna Setup

The last thing you need to do to prepare is to configure your antenna. The provided telescoping antenna works decently well for receiving signals from satellites. For this application, we'll use it in a "v-dipole" configuration. We need each side of the antenna to resonate at 137 MHz—a quick calculation reveals that the proper length for each side is around 54 cm (a quarter of the wavelength of 137 MHz radio waves). Extend your antenna segments to this length, and then fan out each side such that they're separated by 120 degrees. When mounted horizontally, this configuration is great for receiving energy coming from the sky. The radiation pattern is shown in Figure 4-11.

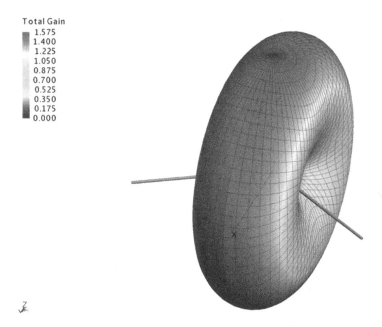

Figure 4-11. *The radiation pattern (gain scaled) of a v-dipole atenna*

I attached my antenna to a long piece of lumber (shown in Figure 4-12); it's helpful to get your antenna off the ground, but if you can't, you can use the tripod and rest your antenna on the ground. Orient in such that the center of the antenna points north. It's also important to do this outside. A building will attenuate the already weak signals coming from the satellite almost 1000 km away.

Figure 4-12. *My rudimentary atenna setup*

Another interesting thing to investigate is placing a metal sheet below your antenna. The function of this is somewhat intuitive—by reflecting energy coming past the antenna back toward it, it will increase the antenna's gain. The effect of placing a large metal sheet beneath the antenna is illustrated in Figure 4-13.

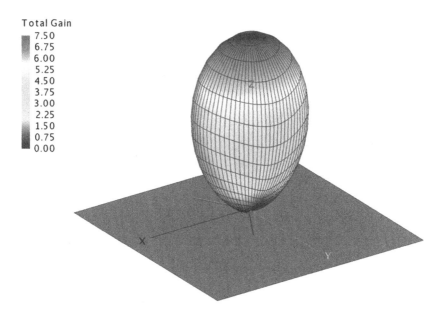

Figure 4-13. *The effect of a metal sheet placed beneath a v-dipole antenna*

Note how energy no longer radiates below the antenna—all the gain in that direction has been "transferred" skyward. You can barely make out the v-dipole in the center of the sheet.

First Flyover

You're now ready for the main event!

1. Select a daytime flyover from the list in WXtoImg; pick one that has a maximum elevation of greater than 50 degrees.

2. Set up your antenna using the preceding information.

3. Configure CubicSDR like before. Ensure that your audio piping program is the output, add a demodulator with a frequency of the one listed in the satellite pass list, and set the bandwidth to 40 kHz.

4. Go back to WXtoImg, and select "Record" from the file menu. Instead of clicking "Manual Test," you should now click "Auto Record," and WXtoImg will wait until the satellite is overhead to start decoding audio.

5. As the satellite comes above the horizon, you should begin to see a faint signal appear on the waterfall plot in CubicSDR. This will look something like the waterfall shown in Figure 4-14.

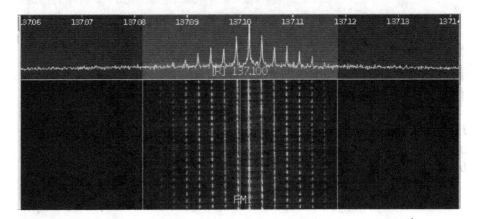

Figure 4-14. *APT signal from a NOAA satellite*

Seeing the faint traces of the satellite's signal appear out of noise for the first time is truly magical—there's a satellite hundreds of miles above you hurtling across the sky, and it's talking to you! You'll notice that the signal appears to slide in frequency throughout the time you can see the signal. This is due to the Doppler shift. As the satellite approaches, its large forward velocity shifts the signal a few kilohertz up. As it recedes, the opposite effect occurs.

Going back to WXtoImg, a view of the sky should appear line by line. There will be two images side by side with some black and white bars. In the daytime, one of the images is visible light and the other is infrared. In the nighttime, both are infrared. The black bars help programs such as WXtoImg align the image later. The black bars also serve as a good indication that you're receiving something. Some images might look like the one in Figure 4-15: almost all noise, with some barely intelligible markings.

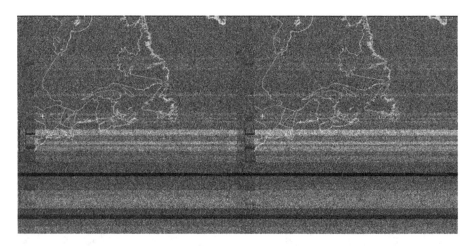

Figure 4-15. *A complete failure; note how it's barely possible to make out the alignment strips on the left in both images. The map is added by WXtoImg in post*

After the flyover, you can mess around with some of WXtoImg's image processing features. In the "Options" menu, you can enable, disable, and align the map overlay featured in my photos. In the "Enhancements" menu, you can have WXtoImg create a false-color combination of the visible light and infrared data. This is only available for some images, as the satellite will need to be transmitting the correct type of data at the time. An example of what you can do with WXtoImg's advanced features is shown in Figure 4-16.

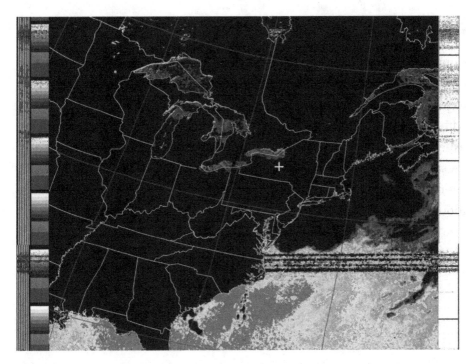

Figure 4-16. *A sea surface temperature map generated using*
WXtoImg

This map uses data from the infrared sensor in addition to location
information to capture the surface temperature of bodies of water in the
image. An interesting feature of note is how portions of the ocean (such
as around New York City) are occluded from the temperature map. This is
because there was a large cloud over the area at the time, and since water
is opaque to infrared radiation, no thermal data from the ocean was able to
reach the sensor. Also note how comparatively cooler the Great Lakes are
than the ocean.

Summary

Congratulations! If all went well, you have now successfully communicated directly with a satellite. I highly recommend exploring WXtoImg further to see what else the program has to offer. Additionally, experimenting with your antenna setup to get the strongest signal possible is a rewarding experience. It's also possible to construct a permanent outdoor antenna for satellite communications; you can find instructions for this online. In a later chapter, we will use an amateur radio satellite to talk with individuals thousands of miles away.

CHAPTER 5

Communications and Modulation

By now, you've read the terms "AM" and "FM" numerous times throughout this text. AM and FM are two common examples of how information is encoded and transmitted using radio waves. As you'll discover, most information cannot be transmitted directly via radio waves. One needs to change the information to make it more suitable for transmission over the air. In this chapter, we'll dive further into common encoding techniques and some of the details behind how modulation and communications systems work.

"Figure 1"

The diagram in Figure 5-1 is so significant that many in the communications industry simply refer to it as Figure 1. Its creator, Claude E. Shannon, is regarded as the father of information theory and modern communications. Shannon provided a mathematical demonstration of how information can be modulated, sent over a channel, and recovered.

© Alex Wulff 2019
A. Wulff, *Beginning Radio Communications*,
https://doi.org/10.1007/978-1-4842-5302-1_5

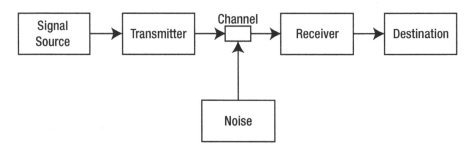

Figure 5-1. *A recreation of Figure 1 from Claude Shannon's*
A Mathematical Theory of Communication

The figure summarizes how Shannon viewed a communications system and how one can view most modern communications systems today. Almost any communications medium, including the electromagnetic spectrum, can be represented as a *channel*. Channels have certain characteristics, such as their ability to propagate information and the noise they add to a message. To communicate over the channel, one utilizes a transmitter. The transmitter's job is to take information and encode it in a certain way that makes it favorable to the channel or the goals of the person/system attempting to transmit the information. A receiver then receives the message over the channel, applies the inverse encoding scheme, and outputs the information stream to its destination.

This separation of the receiver from the destination (in addition to the transmitter from the source) is an extremely powerful concept in modern communications. It enables a single transmitter to accept information from a potentially infinite number of sources. Without this separation, your mobile phone would need a separate transmitter for text, images, audio, and so on. Figure 5-2 demonstrates different ways to represent this information: as a continuous or discrete signal. We'll represent discrete data points in this text as circles with a stem connecting them to the X-axis.

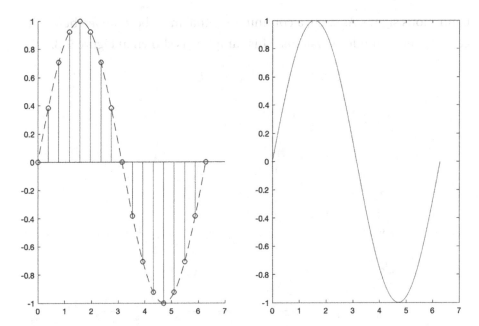

Figure 5-2. *Examples of a discrete signal with a continuous envelope drawn around it (left) and a continuous signal (right)*

Engineers represent information in the form of a *signal*. For our purposes, you can think of a signal as simply values indexed by something. In most cases, this index is time. These values can be continuous, meaning there's no real gap between one value and the next. Despite this lack of a "gap" between values, one can still point at a continuous signal at a particular time and identify its value. For example, one could determine the instantaneous volume of a speaker playing some music.

The other class of signals is *discrete,* meaning that sequential values are separate and distinct. Discrete signals are only defined at particular instants in time (or whatever the index is), and thus their distinct nature makes them very easy to store and manipulate in modern computing devices. In essence, a discrete signal is a list of values. Continuous signals are impossible to store in a regular computer; digital computers deal in the realm of discrete elements of data, so they have no capability to store a continuous signal. As such, a continuous signal must be *sampled* before it can be used in modern systems. This sampling is shown in Figure 5-3.

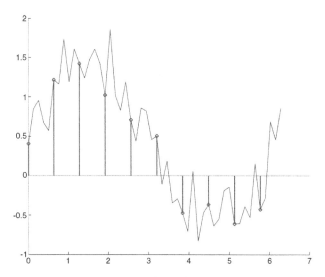

Figure 5-3. *A continuous signal (blue) with its sampled result (red). Notice how some high-frequency information is lost during the sampling process*

To sample a continuous signal, one must decide the rate at which the signal is sampled. A higher sampling rate will require a larger amount of space to store the resulting discrete signal, as there are more samples for a given span of time. However, the resulting discrete signal more closely resembles the continuous signal. A lower sampling rate will require less memory, but has the potential to "miss" information from the original continuous signal. See Figure 5-4 for examples of different sampling rates. This naturally leads to a very important question: does there reach a point where faster sampling becomes redundant? That is, does there exist a sampling rate at which you can perfectly reconstruct the original signal from its samples? Much to the delight of engineers everywhere, the answer is **yes.**

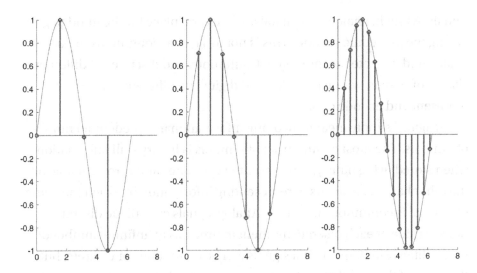

Figure 5-4. *How many samples is too many samples?*

This result is known as the *Shannon-Nyquist Sampling Theorem.*
Shannon mathematically proved that there is no information loss when a
continuous signal is sampled at **twice** the maximum frequency contained
in the signal. A common task that the sampling theorem is well equipped
to help with is sampling and reconstruction of audio. How fast should one
sample audio such that the sampled signal is indistinguishable from the
original? Well, human ears can't really hear frequencies above 20 kHz.
Therefore, a sampling rate of 40 kHz or greater is sufficient to capture
audio. To be clear, information is still lost with a 40 kHz sampling rate,
as tones above 20 kHz cannot be accurately reproduced with a 40 kHz
sampling rate. In the case of audio, this is acceptable because humans
cannot hear these tones anyways.

Analog vs. Digital Information

Throughout this discussion of signals, I have avoided mentioning
analog and digital representations of data. Clear parallels exist between
continuous signals and analog signals, and discrete signals and digital

signals. As such, analog and digital are a natural place for the mind to go during the preceding section. This is not to say that continuous means analog and discrete means digital. Continuous and discrete are different classes of signals, whereas analog and digital are different ways to represent and encode data.

"Digital" simply means encoding information in a predefined number of symbols. The most common set of symbols is binary—all information, when stored using binary, is represented with ones and zeros. Analog, on the other hand, is a means of representing information in which the *value* of a signal is continuous in nature. Analog signals can still be discrete, but the value at each discrete moment in time has an infinite number of possibilities. Similarly, digital signals can be continuous or discrete, but the value of the signal at each moment in time only has a set number of possibilities.

Continuous Analog Signals

The very first information processing was done completely in the realm of continuous analog signals. Long before digital computers existed, engineers utilized analog circuits to process information. This included everything from complex calculations to musical effects for electric guitars. Analog computers were built in this era, but they were slow, large, and expensive due to the lack of generality of various parts of the computer. One analog computer often isn't well suited to a multitude of different tasks (unlike digital computers today). Practically every signal in the natural world is continuous and analog, such as audio, temperatures over time, heartbeats, and more. See Figure 5-5 for an example of a continuous analog signal.

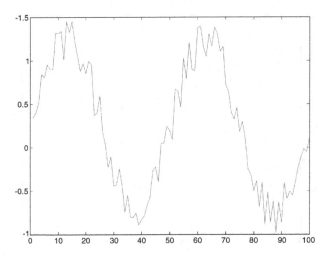

Figure 5-5. *A continuous analog signal*

Discrete Analog Signals

The most common use of discrete analog signals is in digital sampling. Before a continuous analog signal can be converted to binary for use on a computer, it must first be sampled, creating a discrete analog signal. The approximate value of these samples is then converted into binary, forming a discrete digital signal. Information must be lost in this analog-to-binary conversion, as the magnitude of the analog signal can take on an infinite number of values. See Figure 5-6 for an example of a discrete analog signal.

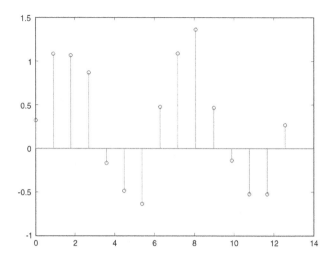

Figure 5-6. *A discrete analog signal. Notice how the discrete samples take on many different values*

These analog samples are often sorted into "bins," with the number of bits for a particular sample determining the number of bins. With one bit you can store two possible values for a given sample, with two bits you can store four possible values, with three bits you can store eight possible values, and so on. This binning process and the resulting reconstruction are shown in Figure 5-7.

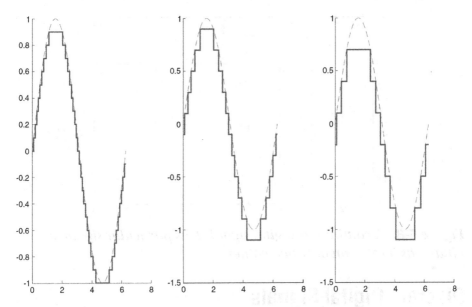

Figure 5-7. *Increasing levels of sampling resolution, or "bins." More bins yield more precise sampling of the original signal*

Continuous Digital Signals

A great example of a continuous digital signal is Morse code. Morse code was transmitted on telegraph lines by completing a circuit and allowing the flow of current across a long wire. Morse code is digital, as it encodes information using "on" or "off" states, but the actual signal transmitting the states is continuous. Any binary signal transmitted over radio waves is another example of a continuous digital signal. See Figure 5-8 for an example of a continuous digital signal.

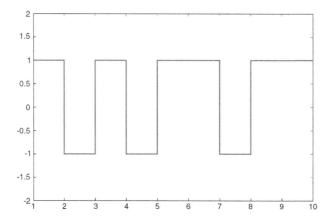

Figure 5-8. *A continuous digital signal. This particular signal is binary, as it takes on only two values*

Discrete Digital Signals

Discrete digital signals power the modern world. Information stored in a computer is discrete and digital; distinct cells in a computer's memory have either a zero or a one stored in them, representing some kind of information. Computers then process this data and store the result as a discrete digital signal. See Figure 5-9 for an example of a discrete digital signal.

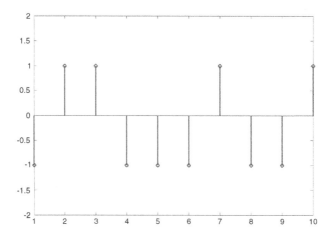

Figure 5-9. *A discrete digital signal that is also binary*

Modulation

You now know the basics of how information is represented in many systems. But this is just half the story of a radio communications system: you now have your data, but how exactly should you send it using radio waves?

By now, we've discussed FM and AM numerous times without actually motivating why AM and FM are necessary in the first place. The answer to this is simply that audio signals, as well as most other signals of interest, do not have favorable characteristics for transmission over a radio channel. As mentioned before, the maximum frequencies audible to human ears are around 20 kHz. If one were to try and feed this audio into an antenna directly, not much would happen.

A good explanation for this is that a resonant antenna in the range of 20 kHz would have to be massive: $300,000,000 \ m/s \div 20,000 \ Hz \approx 15 \ km$. One would need a 15 km-long antenna in order to radiate the power effectively. Additionally, transmitting audio at a different frequency allows for multiple signals to be transmitted at the same time. This is easily seen with radio stations—they all transmit at different frequencies! If all audio signals were transmitted at their original frequencies, it wouldn't be possible to transmit more than one signal at a time. Lastly, you must transmit lower-frequency signals at very high powers in order to get them to propagate effectively.

The solution to these problems is to modulate the original signal on top of some *carrier frequency*. This aptly named carrier frequency carries the information in question at a much higher frequency to its destination. Modulation, as the word is used in the context of communications, generally means encoding information on top of a carrier wave of a different frequency. The next problem that arises is how one can effectively modulate a signal on top of a carrier wave. This can be done by varying one of three properties of a radio wave: *amplitude* (the strength of the signal), *frequency* (the rate at which the signal changes), or *phase* (the relative position of a wave in reference to a standard position). A radio wave can be completely characterized using these three properties.

Amplitude Modulation (AM)

Amplitude modulation is perhaps the easiest modulation technique to understand. For analog signals, the amplitude of the carrier wave, or its envelope, carries the information of the original signal. AM circuits are extremely easy to implement, so amplitude modulation was used to transmit the first messages over radio waves. Figure 5-10 shows how an amplitude-modulated signal appears.

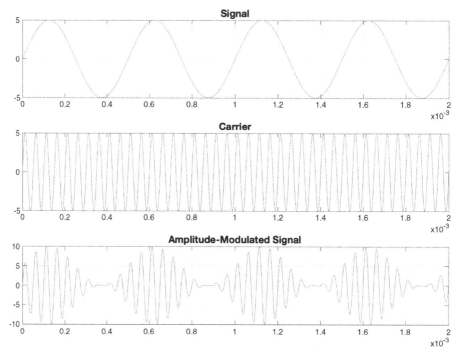

Figure 5-10. *Amplitude modulation: a signal (top) and a carrier (middle) are combined to create an amplitude-modulated signal (bottom)*

The digital version of amplitude modulation is called *amplitude-shift keying (ASK)*. This generally involves switching a carrier wave between differing, discrete amplitude states. Amplitude-modulated signals are very susceptible to noise. The presence of noise generally affects the amplitude of a radio wave at the receiver, and since the signal is encoded in the carrier's amplitude, this can obscure the original message.

Frequency Modulation (FM)

Frequency modulation of analog signals involves changing the frequency of the carrier wave based on the amplitude of the signal. This is best illustrated in the following image. FM is much less prone to noise than AM because random noise does not affect the frequency of the wave. Circuits to implement FM are more difficult to produce and understand than AM; as such, FM did not come into use until decades after AM. See Figure 5-11 for an example of frequency modulation.

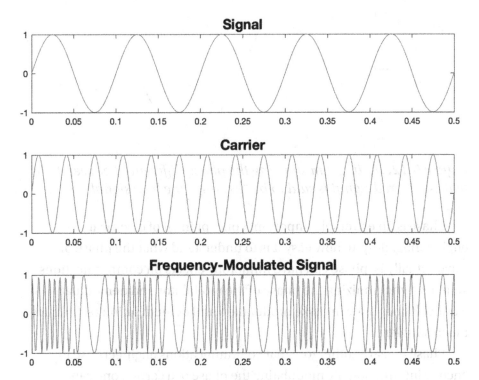

Figure 5-11. *A frequency-modulated signal: the original signal is on the top, the carrier is in the middle, and the result is on the bottom. As the signal's amplitude increases, so does the frequency of the carrier*

The digital counterpart to analog frequency modulation is *frequency-shift keying*, in which the carrier is modulated between a set number of frequencies. Each frequency can encode a different piece of information.

Phase Modulation

The phase of a wave represents its offset to a reference phase. This concept is best illustrated with an image, such as the one in Figure 5-12 showing different phase offsets for a sine wave.

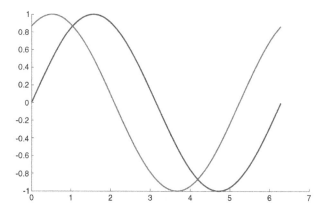

Figure 5-12. *A diagram showing the phase difference between two waves. The red signal is said to be "leading" the blue signal*

Phase is an extremely important concept in all of electrical engineering; despite how easy it is to understand what the phase of a wave actually is, phase can have numerous effects on communications systems. Synchronizing the phase of the modulator and demodulator is a difficult task, but can make modulation and demodulation techniques much simpler.

Phase is also another tool that communications engineers use to encode information. By modulating the phase of a carrier, one can encode information in a similar manner to modulation of frequency and amplitude. Phase modulation is almost always used to encode digital information rather than analog; this is done in the form of phase-shift keying (PSK), which is shown in Figure 5-13.

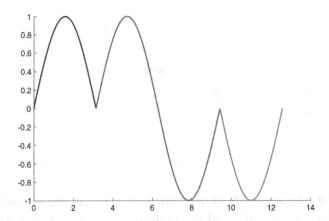

Figure 5-13. *Binary phase modulation: the phase of the carrier is modulated 180 degrees to indicate a binary 1 or a binary 0. Changes in color of the signal indicate a change in the bit*

Frequency Division

A fascinating—and underappreciated—result of utilizing waves of different frequencies to encode information is their ability to be transmitted at the same time over the same channel and then subsequently recovered. This important principle is what enables all modern forms of radio communication. Transmitting information on different carrier frequencies at the same time is known as *frequency multiplexing*. The alternative to frequency multiplexing is *time multiplexing,* or transmitting information on the same carrier frequency at different times. Time multiplexing is shown in Figure 5-14.

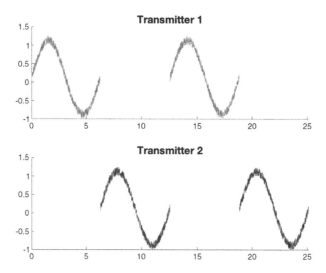

Figure 5-14. *An example of time multiplexing, where two separate transmitters each get allotted a certain amount of time to transmit before switching. Time is represented on the horizontal axis in this figure*

It's very easy to see how frequency multiplexing can be more efficient. Imagine 1000 people in a room attempting to carry out a conversation with 1000 other people. It would be next to impossible to hear your conversation over the conversations of others, so everyone would be forced to take turns speaking. Now imagine that each pair of people is in a separate room—no turns have to be taken, and everyone can speak at once. In this scenario, the separate rooms represent separate carrier frequencies.

2G cellular networks used a time multiplexing scheme for data and voice services. This vastly limited data rates but was easier to implement with the hardware of the time. This technology, known as GSM, is still in use throughout many portions of the world. 4G LTE data services use a frequency multiplexing scheme with many channels allocated for each phone that vastly increases data transfer speeds.

The word channel in the topic of frequency division refers to a specific slice of frequencies allotted to a transmitter. This can be confusing, as the word channel is also used to describe a general communications medium (which is how I have mostly used to this point). The meaning of channel is generally clear from context. As you might expect, channel width varies with application. AM radio was originally designed to transmit voice signals across large swaths of area; as such, channels are only 10 kHz. This greatly limits the quality of the audio, making AM not a great option for transmitting music. FM channels are 200 kHz—this enables FM radio stations to transmit high-quality stereo audio. In fact, analog FM radio will oftentimes sound better than many digital radio streams from satellite radio or from the Internet.

Quadrature Encoding

It's even possible to transmit two waves of the same frequency at the same time, provided that certain conditions are met. This is called quadrature encoding. This allows the data rate of a particular channel to increase even further—in fact, quadrature encoding is utilized in many of the newest high-data-transfer-rate communications schemes.

The two waves can be summed, transmitted at the same time, and then recovered as long as they're 90 degrees out of phase. Sine and cosine waves are separated by 90 degrees, so it's common to refer to the two carriers as the sine and cosine portions of the data transmission scheme. The sine component is often referred to as the "in phase" portion, and the 90-degree-shifted cosine component is often referred to as the "quadrature" portion. This is where quadrature encoding/modulation gets its name.

The most commonly implemented form of quadrature encoding is Quadrature Amplitude Modulation, or QAM. QAM is so efficient at transferring data that it is utilized in 4G LTE and 5G technologies to transfer information. In QAM, the intensity of the in phase and quadrature carriers is independently modulated to encode a series of bits. At the receiver, the two carriers are separated, and their levels are decoded. Different combinations of levels of each carrier can represent a string of bits. If more levels are used, more bits can be encoded in a single state of the sine and cosine waves. Figure 5-15 is your first glimpse into QAM: the constellation diagram.

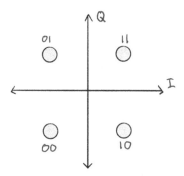

Figure 5-15. *A constellation diagram depicting different levels of the I and Q carriers mapped to different binary values*

QAM is easy to understand through the use of a constellation diagram. The constellation diagram shows the relative level of the I and Q carriers and how they map to different sequences of bits. The preceding constellation diagram shows a 4-QAM communications setup. It is given this name because there are four possible symbols; to achieve this, two levels of voltage must be used for each carrier. This is also made clear in the constellation plot, as it shows possible levels of +/- V for the received intensity of the I and Q portions (where V is some arbitrary voltage level). The *symbol rate* is the rate at which these changes in voltages of the carriers occur. To transmit more information using QAM, one can increase the number of voltage levels used to convey information. This allows for more possible combinations of the levels of the two carriers, consequently transmitting more bits per symbol. A higher-order QAM scheme is shown in Figure 5-16.

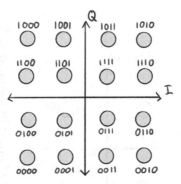

Figure 5-16. *A 16-QAM constellation diagram. Each carrier now has four possible different levels as opposed to the two that 4-QAM requires*

Some 5G standards even call for the use of 256-QAM which can allow data transfer rates in excess of 1 billion bits (Gbits) per second with a sufficiently fast symbol rate. One might ask, "Then, why don't communications engineers keep extending QAM even farther?" The answer to this question is *noise*. There does exist a finite maximum level for the signal intensity, so to keep adding intensity levels to QAM, engineers must subdivide the maximum range into more and more discrete levels. Noise can then make one level appear like another, introducing errors in the communication scheme. Modern implementations of quadrature encoding apply a sophisticated means to correct for errors, but this only works to a certain extent. This idea of noise is shown in Figure 5-17. Red dots in this figure represent received QAM signals—as noise increases, it becomes harder to classify signals. This problem is compounded by adding more levels of QAM. You can imagine that if instead of one symbol per quadrant there were two symbols per quadrant, it would be even harder to identify where a particular signal is supposed to fall.

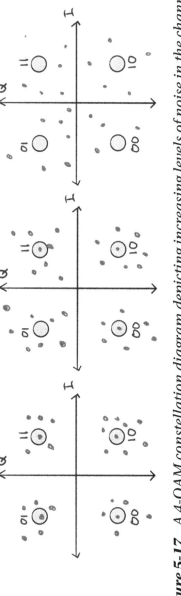

Figure 5-17. A 4-QAM constellation diagram depicting increasing levels of noise in the channel

Summary

Hopefully this chapter shed a little more light on how information is transmitted using radio waves and general communications channels. Information can be continuous or discrete, and represented in a digital or analog fashion. Modulation is then used to encode this information on a carrier wave. A carrier wave makes such data more favorable for transmission across a channel. One can modulate three things about an electromagnetic wave: its amplitude, frequency, and phase. With these three components, you can completely characterize a radio wave, and each can be used to modulate data.

You actually now have a somewhat complete, albeit high-level, picture of what a radio communications setup looks like. Understanding the interplay between the realm of information/data and the physical devices and principles that transmit this information is very important; if there's something you don't understand, be sure to go back and read it again and/or do more of your own research! In the next chapter, we'll utilize a device called a *microcontroller* to send and receive packets of information using radio devices. This will allow you to put some of the things learned in this chapter into practice.

CHAPTER 6

Exploring Radio

While you're waiting to take your licensing test, you can read this chapter and complete the exercises to learn more about how radio technology can be applied in the world of digital communications. The weather satellite chapter (Chapter 4) may have been your first experience directly receiving a radio transmission, but in this chapter, you will gain a deeper insight into how radio communication also serves as a great opportunity to explore how various obstacles in the path of radio waves can affect signal quality and strength. The setup we'll use is shown in Figure 6-1. If you have not yet purchased the materials for this chapter, now is a good time to review the list in Chapter 1 and do so.

© Alex Wulff 2019
A. Wulff, *Beginning Radio Communications*,
https://doi.org/10.1007/978-1-4842-5302-1_6

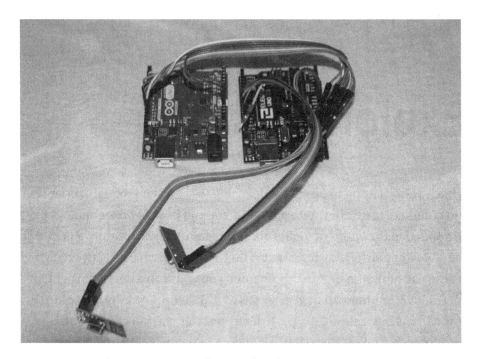

Figure 6-1. *The microcontroller and radio setup used in this chapter*

The larger blue and black boards are two versions of the same microcontroller, and the two smaller boards at the bottom of the photo are the radio modules connected to a microcontroller with jumper wires. Two separate microcontroller/radio pairs are used in this project.

Microcontrollers

A microcontroller is a small device designed to execute instructions. Microcontrollers are similar to computers in that they interpret computer code to accomplish tasks, but microcontrollers are generally constrained to complete very specific tasks. They execute instructions many orders of magnitude slower than a typical computer processor, and oftentimes only have one processing core, rendering them inefficient for doing multiple things at once. Despite these limitations, microcontrollers are easy to program and operate, and it's simple to use them with various radio modules.

A microcontroller normally has a microprocessor which actually executes the instructions and various supporting peripherals such as devices to regulate power supply, status lights, oscillators, and more. A typical microcontroller is shown in Figure 6-2. This particular variant of a microcontroller is manufactured by a company called Arduino. Arduino produces various hardware devices for hobbyists that are easy to learn how to program. Before Arduino, programming microcontrollers was left to industry professionals with years of experience. Arduino also produces software to allow individuals to program their microcontrollers with ease—this software has been adapted to support the programming of hundreds of different microcontroller designs produced by many different companies. We'll use Arduino software later to program the microcontrollers used in this chapter.

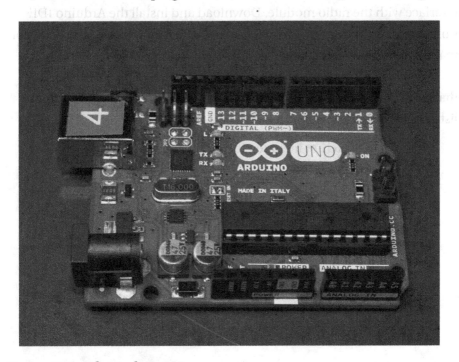

Figure 6-2. *The Arduino Uno*

The radio modules we'll use are capable and inexpensive devices commonly used by hobbyists. They offer a transmit range of a few hundred feet and operate in the unlicensed 2.4 GHz radio band (the same band shared by Wi-Fi routers, microwave ovens, and many other devices). These particular devices utilize the NRF24L01 chipset.

The Arduino IDE

First, we'll download the Arduino software that we'll use to program the microcontroller. This software is an IDE, or integrated development environment. IDEs generally contain all the pieces necessary to help a programmer write software, then compile it and deploy it on a device. The Arduino IDE supports external libraries, or collections of software that enable support for a specific function. In this case, we'll use a library to interface with the radio module. Download and install the Arduino IDE from `www.arduino.cc/en/Main/Software`. The Arduino IDE is available on macOS, Windows, and Linux.

Now that you have the IDE installed, we'll need to install the library that allows us to interface with the radio module. The steps to do this are listed as follows:

1. Go to Sketch ➤ Include Library ➤ Manage Libraries (as shown in Figure 6-3).

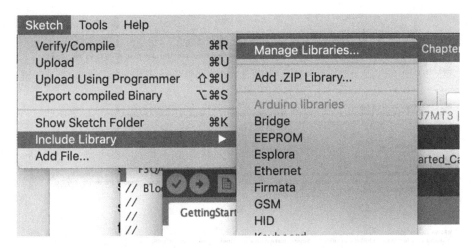

Figure 6-3. *The menu option to open the library manager*

2. Search "RF24" in the window that appears, and find the library named "RF24" (by user TMRh20). You may need to scroll down.

3. Click the library, and then click the install button. Select the most recent version from the dropdown. This step is shown in Figure 6-4.

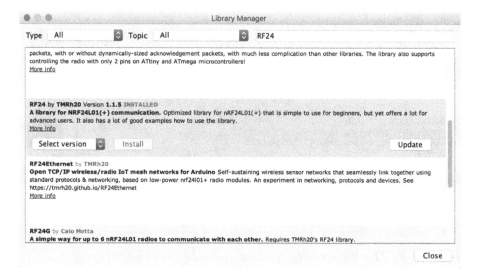

Figure 6-4. *The library manager screen with the RF24 library selected. Mine looks slightly different because I already have the library installed*

RF24 is a library that makes it easy to interface with the NRF24L01 radio modules. This library contains collections of software that provide a simple code-based interface to initialize the radio modules, change various settings, and send/receive packets of data.

The Code

The microcontrollers themselves do nothing without instruction; microcontrollers need code to execute in order to be useful. We'll use separate code for each microcontroller. One will act as a "server" to serve messages, and another will act as a "client" that receives the messages and sends a response. This network model is common across many communications systems, such as with the servers that power much of the Internet.

I have created software for this chapter that you can download from www.AlexWulff.com/radiobook/code.zip. Your computer should automatically download the file. After downloading, unzip the file and extract its contents to a directory of your choosing. Inside are two folders, "Client" and "Server." Inside each of these folders is a file of the same name ending in ".ino". This is the file extension that Arduino expects its software to have—double-clicking a .ino file opens up the Arduino IDE automatically. You can also open .ino files in Arduino by going to File ➤ Open. Arduino-compatible software, or a "sketch" as it's called, is written in C++. C++ is a popular programming language; if you're familiar with it, you'll have no trouble understanding the sketches used in this chapter. Listings 6-1 and 6-2 provide the sketches for reference.

Listing 6-1. Server.ino

```
// Code created by Alex Wulff
// www.AlexWulff.com

#include <SPI.h>
#include <RF24.h>

// CE, CSN
RF24 radio(9, 10);
int packetID = 0;

const byte addresses[][6] = { "server", "client" };

void setup() {
  Serial.begin(9600);
  radio.begin();
  radio.openWritingPipe(addresses[1]);
  radio.openReadingPipe(1,addresses[0]);
  radio.setPALevel(RF24_PA_MIN);
}

void loop() {
  packetID++; char message[50];
  sprintf(message,"Packet ID: %d",packetID);
```

```
unsigned long sendTime = micros();
radio.stopListening();
bool stat = radio.write(&message, sizeof(message));
if (stat == 0) {Serial.println("TX Failed!");}
else {Serial.print("Sent Packet ID: "); Serial.
println(packetID);}

delay(5);
radio.startListening();

bool timeout = false;
while(!radio.available()) {
  if (micros() - sendTime > 300000) {
    timeout = true;
    Serial.println("Receive Timeout!");
    break;
  }
}

if (!timeout) {
  char received[50];
  radio.read(&received, sizeof(received));
  unsigned long roundTripTime = micros() - sendTime;

  Serial.print("ACK Round Trip Time: ");
  Serial.print(roundTripTime);
  Serial.print(" | Message: ");
  Serial.println(received);
}

delay(500);
}
```

The server sketch attempts to send a message and then listens for a reply from the client. If a certain period of time elapses before the server receives a message from the client, the server will time out and attempt to send a message again.

Listing 6-2. Client.ino

```
#include <SPI.h>
#include <RF24.h>

// CE, CSN
RF24 radio(9, 10);
int packetID = 0;

const byte addresses[][6] ={ "server", "client" };

void setup() {
  Serial.begin(9600);
  radio.begin();
  radio.openReadingPipe(1, addresses[1]);
  radio.openWritingPipe(addresses[0]);
  radio.setPALevel(RF24_PA_MIN);
}

void loop() {
  packetID++; delay(10);
  radio.startListening();

  if (radio.available()){
    char received[32] = "";
    radio.read(&received, sizeof(received));
    Serial.println(received);
  }

  delay(5);
```

```
  radio.stopListening();
  char toSend[32];
  sprintf(toSend,"Receiver ACK: %d",packetID) ;
  radio.write(&toSend, sizeof(toSend));
  delay(500);
}
```

The client sketch will wait until it receives a message and then send a response back to the server. We'll now wire the circuit, then come back to these sketches.

The Radio Module

As mentioned before, the radio module utilizes the NRF24L01 2.4 GHz radio transceiver. This integrated circuit is inexpensive and well supported with many different software libraries. The NRF24L01 chip does not occupy much space on the module—the rest of the hardware is supporting equipment necessary for the transmission and reception of data. The radio module also includes a 2.4 GHz antenna in the form of a trace antenna. Trace antennas occupy an extremely small amount of space and can be manufactured directly on a printed circuit board with minimal to no changes to manufacturing hardware. Trace antennas have the highest directional gain to electromagnetic waves hitting the circuit board perpendicularly. Other components on the board include a 16 MHz oscillator (a crystal that produces a signal with a frequency of 16 MHz) as well as various resistors and capacitors to regulate power.

Microcontrollers interface with this module using a digital communications standard called Serial Peripheral Interface (SPI). In SPI, a "master" microcontroller controls "slave" peripheral devices. SPI communication requires a clock line to synchronize communications, two data lines to actually transmit messages, and a select line to select which slave device is active. This module also has lines for power and ground and a special line to enable transmitting/receiving. In total, you will make seven connections between the Arduino and the radio module.

The Circuit

We'll make electrical connections between the radio module and your Arduino device using *jumper wires*, which are wires with connectors that interface well with various modules and microcontrollers. The jumper wires used in this chapter are listed in the "Materials" section of Chapter 1.

Jumper wires have a male and a female connector. The female connector connects to the exposed metal pins on the radio module, and the male connector gets plugged into the receptacles on the body of the microcontroller.

Figure 6-5 lists each of the pins on the radio module. We'll decode these below, although you don't really need to know what each does for the purposes of this chapter:

- "GND" is the ground pin for the radio module.

- "VCC" is the positive voltage supply pin for the radio module (expected to be around 3.3 V).

- "CE" is the chip-enable pin.

- "CSN" is the chip-select line that activates the radio module.

- "SCK" is the SPI clock line.

- "MOSI" is the master-out-slave-in line, which the microcontroller uses to send data to the radio module.

- "MISO" is the master-in-slave-out line, which the radio module uses to send data to the microcontroller.

- "IRQ" is an interrupt pin that we will not use in this example.

1: GND   2: VCC
3: CE   4: CSN
5: SCK   6: MOSI
7: MISO 8: IRQ

Figure 6-5. *A listing of the pins on the radio module*

Now that you know what each of the pins on the radio module is, you can begin to connect them to the microcontroller with the jumper wires. The connections you'll need to make are listed in Figure 6-6. For example, the figure indicates that you need to connect the VCC pin to the 3V3 pin, as the VCC label is next to the 3V3 pin.

A radio communications system is useless with just one radio— make the same connections to another radio module with the second microcontroller as you do the first, so you have a pair of transceivers.

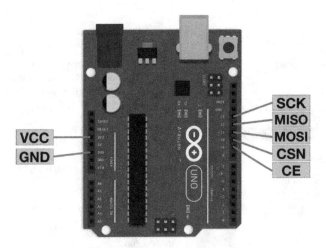

Figure 6-6. *What connections to make with the microcontroller*

If you did everything correctly, those should be the last connections you need to make. All the tinkering from here on out will be entirely software based! You can now go ahead and connect one of the boards to your computer via the included USB cable. Various lights should come on on the microcontroller as it powers up.

The Arduino IDE needs to know what board you're using. With the Client.ino sketch open, go to Tools ➤ Board ➤ Arduino/Genuino Uno. This is shown in Figure 6-7. Your board window will likely look different than mine.

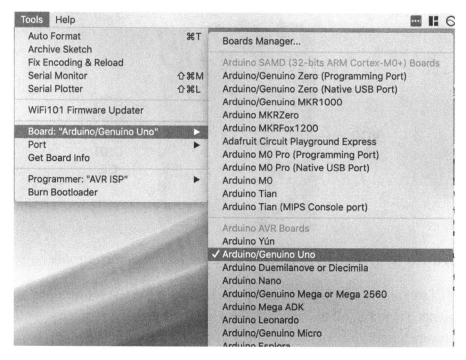

Figure 6-7. *Arduino IDE board selection menu*

Next, the Arduino IDE needs to know what port on your computer the board is attached to. Go to Tools ➤ Port, and select your Uno. On macOS, it should appear similar to the port shown in Figure 6-8. On Windows, the board will be listed as something similar to "COM3 (Arduino/Genuino Uno)." The number after "COM" will likely be different.

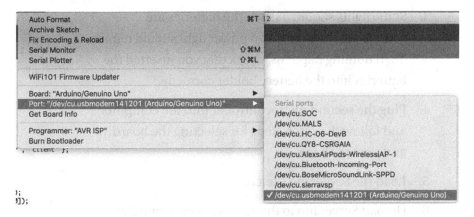

Figure 6-8. Arduino IDE port selection menu

All the necessary settings should now be configured. Ensure that the Client.ino sketch is open, and click the "Upload" button at the top-left corner of the screen (this looks like an arrow pointing to the right).

During uploading, the lights on your microcontroller will flash, and the sketch will finish uploading after a few seconds. If you unplug and plug the microcontroller back in, this sketch will remain in the microcontroller's memory, and it will begin executing the sketch from the beginning. There's no need to ever reprogram the microcontroller unless you want to change something about the sketch.

If you encounter any issues with programming, Arduino has a support article online to help: `www.arduino.cc/en/guide/troubleshooting#toc1`. Common issues include not having the correct port selected and not having the correct board selected. We'll now upload the server sketch to the other microcontroller.

1. Unplug the first microcontroller from the computer.

2. Place AA batteries in the battery pack, and then plug the battery pack into the connector on the microcontroller that you just unplugged from the computer.

3. Some lights should flash as the batteries are
    connected, then the green power light should remain
    on. If nothing happens, check that you inserted the
    batteries into the battery holder correctly.

4. Plug the second microcontroller into the computer,
    and follow the same steps for selecting the board
    and port as above.

5. Load the Server.ino sketch.

6. Upload Server.ino to the second microcontroller.

You should now have two programmed microcontrollers with radio
modules attached. The microcontroller with the Client.ino sketch should
be powered by batteries and disconnected from the computer. The
microcontroller with the Server.ino sketch should be connected to the
computer.

We'll now verify that your setup is working. The Arduino IDE has
something called a serial monitor that can receive information from
the microcontroller. Every time "Serial.print" gets called in the code,
information is sent to the serial monitor. This serial monitor is an easy way
to verify that everything is working correctly. To open the serial monitor,
click the icon at the upper-right corner of the IDE. This is shown in
Figure 6-9.

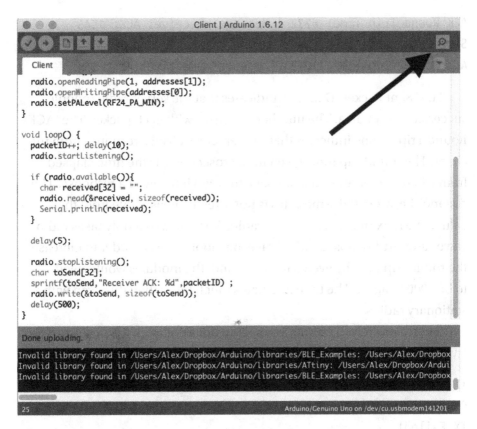

```
radio.openReadingPipe(1, addresses[1]);
radio.openWritingPipe(addresses[0]);
radio.setPALevel(RF24_PA_MIN);
}

void loop() {
  packetID++; delay(10);
  radio.startListening();

  if (radio.available()){
    char received[32] = "";
    radio.read(&received, sizeof(received));
    Serial.println(received);
  }

  delay(5);

  radio.stopListening();
  char toSend[32];
  sprintf(toSend,"Receiver ACK: %d",packetID) ;
  radio.write(&toSend, sizeof(toSend));
  delay(500);
}
```

```
Done uploading.

Invalid library found in /Users/Alex/Dropbox/Arduino/libraries/BLE_Examples: /Users/Alex/Dropbox
Invalid library found in /Users/Alex/Dropbox/Arduino/libraries/ATtiny: /Users/Alex/Dropbox/Ardui
Invalid library found in /Users/Alex/Dropbox/Arduino/libraries/BLE_Examples: /Users/Alex/Dropbox
```

Figure 6-9. How to open the Arduino IDE's serial monitor

When the microcontrollers are correctly sending data to one another, an output such as the one in the following should appear in the serial monitor:

```
Sent Packet ID: 1551
ACK Round Trip Time: 8776 | Message: Receiver ACK: 1542
Sent Packet ID: 1552
ACK Round Trip Time: 8772 | Message: Receiver ACK: 1543
Sent Packet ID: 1553
ACK Round Trip Time: 8776 | Message: Receiver ACK: 1544
Sent Packet ID: 1554
```

```
ACK Round Trip Time: 8772 | Message: Receiver ACK: 1545
Sent Packet ID: 1555
ACK Round Trip Time: 10724 | Message: Receiver ACK: 1546
```

The "Sent Packet ID ..." line indicates that the server radio module successfully sent data. The number increases with each packet. The "ACK Round Trip ..." line indicates that the server received a response from the client. The round trip time, given in microseconds, is the time elapsed from when the server sent a message to when it received a response. The distance between radio modules is not directly measurable from this value. The maximum range of the radios is small, and it only takes radio waves around 1 nanosecond to travel one foot. Thus, in order to increase the round trip time by even a microsecond, the modules would need to be 1000 ft. apart. The time fluctuates much more than this even with stationary radios.

It's also entirely likely that your setup does not work the first time you try it. An unsuccessful output will look similar to the one as follows:

```
TX Failed!
Receive Timeout!
TX Failed!
Receive Timeout!
TX Failed!
Receive Timeout!
TX Failed!
```

The line "TX Failed!" indicates that the radio module was unsuccessful in sending data to the other microcontroller. If the connections are incorrect between the microcontroller and the radio, you may receive this message. Or, if the connections are incorrect, you might not get any message at all. If something isn't working, double- and triple-check all of the connections on both devices.

You can also get "TX Failed!" if the two radios are out of range. The RF24 library automatically resends each message a certain number of times if the other radio module doesn't respond to indicate that the transmission was successful. This response is not handled in the client or server sketches; instead, the library does this behind the scenes. If the number of automatic resends elapses without a response, the RF24 library will indicate that a transmission failed.

"TX Failed!" is also accompanied by "Receive Timeout!" in the serial monitor output. The server sketch waits a certain period of time to receive a response before attempting to send a message to the client again. If this period of time elapses, the microcontroller will print the timeout message and attempt to send a message again.

The client sketch also has serial output. If you're curious, you can connect the server to the battery pack and connect the client to the computer and observe its serial output. In order for the serial monitor to appear correctly, the microcontroller must be selected in the Arduino IDE's port selection setting.

Experimentation

Now that the setup is out of the way, you can begin to experiment! Unfortunately, the RF24 library has no means of indicating the signal strength of received messages. Signal strength is a great way to observe how changes you make affect the communications system. A measurable quantity that allows you to indirectly observe signal strength is the round trip time. If the two radios are far enough apart, it will take many attempts to send the message and wait for a response before a message and acknowledgement gets through. This entire process takes time, so you will see an increase in round trip time due to this acknowledgement procedure as the radios move apart.

You can expect round trip times of less than 10,000 microseconds when the modules are close to one another and times between 10,000 and 40,000 microseconds when the modules are far apart.

The first thing I recommend trying is exploring the range of the pair of radios. You can do this by taking the client and placing it at increasing distances from the server until the connection drops completely. There's no indication on the client of whether or not it's connected to the server, so you'll need to go back to your computer to see the status of the link. If you're using a laptop, you can leave the client and carry the laptop around to see how the signal changes.

This is a good opportunity to explore antenna radiation patterns as well. Once you're at the point where the signal drops out, try twisting the radio module in different ways to see if you can regain the connection. As mentioned, the antenna on the radio module has the highest gain to signals perpendicular the board. You will likely not observe any effects of polarization—rotating the board on some axes will have no effect. The signals from this board will appear cross-polarized, meaning the radio waves hitting the receiver are polarized both vertically and horizontally. The dominant effect here is the radiation pattern of the antenna.

Try placing obstacles in the path of the signal, and see how it changes signal reception. You can go so far as to almost completely wrap a radio module in tinfoil and still receive a signal. The small amount of energy that leaks out of the gaps in the tinfoil can still carry a signal to the other radio, as you will observe. If you try wrapping a radio in tinfoil, make sure that you surround it with paper first. The tinfoil can cause problems by shorting the metal contacts on the radio.

Software Modifications

These radios contain hardware called a power amplifier that can boost the power of the signal emitted from the radio. The level of amplification is software configurable. The client and server sketches set this amplification to the minimum possible level in the line shown as follows:

```
radio.setPALevel(RF24_PA_MIN);
```

You can modify the RF24_PA_MIN value to one of the following options:

- RF24_PA_MIN

- RF24_PA_LOW

- RF24_PA_HIGH

- RF24_PA_MAX

The power difference between MIN and MAX is obviously the greatest, so I recommend only switching between those two options. If you modify a sketch, you will need to save the sketch and re-upload it to the microcontroller. If you change the power level, you'll need to do it on both microcontrollers to observe any changes.

If you're comfortable with software, you can configure many more options on the radio such as data rate and auto-acknowledgement and see how these affect range. A full list of options is available on the RF24 library page: https://tmrh20.github.io/RF24/classRF24.html.

Summary

If all went well, you just implemented your first communications network! This small network is comprised of microcontrollers—processors that execute simple instructions—and radio modules. We programmed these microcontrollers through the Arduino IDE, using a library designed to facilitate communications with the radio modules.

This network is more of a proof of concept rather than a useful communications system. Data is sent for the purpose of exploring radio propagation and its effects. One would use these radio modules for any application that requires a short-range data link. They're even capable of supporting data rates in excess of 1 million bits per second (Mbps), which is fast enough to transfer images in a reasonable amount of time.

It's worth your time to try and expand these radios to fit a different application. The Arduino platform is a powerful way to explore radio communications, IoT, sensing, and so much more. There are numerous resources available that make it easy to learn how to create interesting projects with Arduino-based devices. In the next chapter, we'll explore the world of amateur radio and how you can go about obtaining an amateur radio license.

CHAPTER 7

Amateur Radio

You may have heard the term "ham radio" before; in this chapter, we will explore what exactly amateur, or "ham," radio is and how you can get involved in it.

What Is It?

The best way to describe amateur radio is as a *community*. Amateur radio operators, or "hams" as they're called, are individuals with an interest in radio that utilize special frequency allocations to do interesting things. All amateur radio operators have a special license to operate in these bands. In most countries, this license is obtained by taking a test. In the United States, the Federal Communications Commission (FCC) oversees this test and what bands are allocated to hams. According to the FCC, there are around 750,000 licensed hams in the United States alone. Most other countries have a similar governing body, with the International Telecommunication Union (ITU) generally providing direction for all countries. The ITU divides the world into three separate regions for administrative purposes, as shown in Figure 7-1.

© Alex Wulff 2019
A. Wulff, *Beginning Radio Communications*,
https://doi.org/10.1007/978-1-4842-5302-1_7

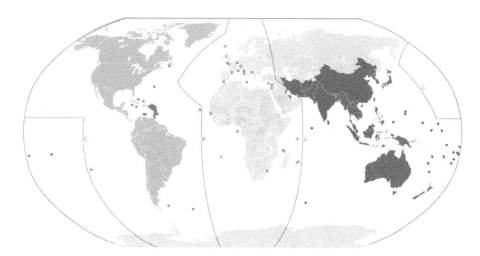

Figure 7-1. *The ITU's designation of different regions of the world. Separate designations are created to facilitate management of the electromagnetic spectrum*

Amateur radio operators have many different reasons for participating in the hobby. Some enjoy talking with other operators thousands of miles away, some enjoy volunteering in events that utilize hams for communications, while some want to be prepared in case disaster strikes and normal communications modes are down. Clearly, there are many creative ways to utilize the frequency bands allotted for amateur radio. Many hams operate amateur radio from stations called "shacks" like the one in Figure 7-2, but in this text, we'll utilize a small, portable radio to contact others.

Figure 7-2. *An amateur radio "shack" with a variety of different radios and computers. Image from* `https://commons.wikimedia.org/wiki/File:MwOrkbshack.jpg`

Another key part of amateur radio is that communications on amateur frequencies cannot be used for commercial purposes. This is why amateur radio is called "amateur." Hams cannot be paid for their services on amateur radio bands, and there are very stringent requirements about the type of content that can be transmitted. These requirements include rules like "you can't transmit music on amateur frequencies" and "very few communications can be encrypted." The purpose of amateur radio is to allow for disaster communications, citizen communications, education, event organization, and more. These goals would not be achievable if ham bands were polluted with commercial traffic.

Frequency Allocations

Certain frequency slices are allotted to amateur radio operators across the entire radio spectrum. These slices are referred to as "bands," and are generally classified by a band's wavelength. Different bands are more suitable for different tasks, primarily due to the physical properties of lower- and higher-frequency radio waves that you're already familiar with.

Lower-frequency bands such as 40-meter, 30-meter, 20-meter, and 10-meter are used to make long-distance contacts with large setups. These bands require large antennas that are generally not well suited for mobile operation. The 2 m and 70 cm bands are popular for newer operators, as much less equipment is necessary to transmit and receive on these bands. This comes at a cost, however, as the these shorter wavelengths only travel in the line-of-sight propagation mode.

Longer-wavelength bands can exploit special properties of the Earth's atmosphere to travel great distances. Transmissions in longer bands can be bounced off the upper levels of the atmosphere to communicate with individuals across oceans. The atmosphere can also serve as a "waveguide" that allows signals to propagate across the globe. These phenomena are generally time or season dependent, so certain bands are only active at certain times. Solar activity also impacts atmospheric communications—solar flares and coronal mass ejections can both enhance and hinder various communications modes. The US frequency allocation chart, as mentioned earlier, is a great resource for examining bands allocated to amateur radio operators. Figure 7-3 shows a few of these bands.

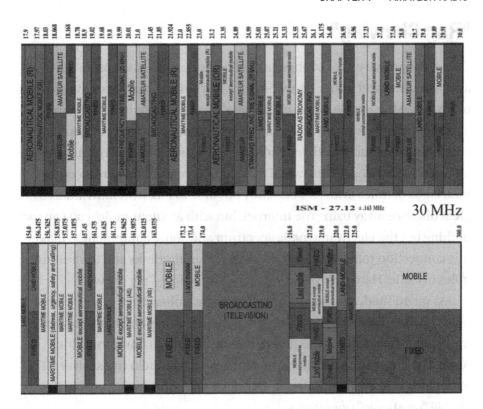

Figure 7-3. *A small section of the US frequency allocation chart*

The dark-green sections are amateur radio bands, some of which are also used for amateur radio satellite communications (light green). Frequency allocations listed are from 18 to 30 MHz and from 154 to 300 MHz.

Uses of Amateur Radio

You now have a better idea of what bands are available to hams, but it's amateur radio operators doing interesting things on these bands that makes amateur radio so special. The following sections provide a snapshot of some of the common use cases for amateur radio.

"Rag Chewing"

One of the primary uses of amateur radio frequencies is simply to have a conversation with other hams. Such conversations can be conducted over voice, Morse code, or another digital format. The interesting part about communicating on amateur radio frequencies is that you can communicate directly with individuals across the globe. There's an incredibly satisfying feeling when making a direct or semi-direct contact thousands of miles away. It's certainly possible to talk with individuals a great distance away using the Internet, but with amateur radio, you can use nothing but the electromagnetic spectrum and some equipment to make this connection rather than hundreds of server interlinks and thousands of miles of cable. Hams call these longer conversations "rag chews."

As mentioned, amateur radio operators will often have a "shack" that holds one's equipment and antennas. Large antennas and high-powered transmitters are generally required for long-distance communications. Almost all amateur radio operators also have a handheld transceiver (HT) for shorter-range and mobile communications. Some even have car rigs to enable "on-the-go" operations.

Contests

Hams also enjoy participating in various forms of contests. A common form of contest is to make as many contacts from as many cities, states, or countries as possible within a certain amount of time. Upon making a contact, each station would enter the other's identifier (more on this later) to officially record the contact. Many individuals take pride in achieving extremely long-distance contacts, as this demonstrates radio prowess. Some hams attempt to make long-distance contacts using limited hardware, which makes the task even more challenging.

Other contests can be more local in nature. A particularly interesting one is where an individual hides a transmitter in an undisclosed location and others try and hunt the transmitter using directional antennas. The first individual to find the hidden transmitter is declared the winner.

Regardless of contest type, contest organizers oftentimes issue certificates to stations that achieve a certain number of contacts. Such a certificate is shown in Figure 7-4.

Figure 7-4. *A certificate issued to the Harvard Wireless Club for performing well in a national contest. The author was one of the operators of Harvard Wireless Club during this contest*

Emergency Communications

One of the more practical uses of amateur radio bands is for communications during times of emergency. In fact, many amateur radio contests are designed to strengthen hams' skills in the event that disaster strikes. Hurricanes, earthquakes, and terrorist attacks can result in a complete communications blackout. Direct radio links are often the only practical means of communication left in such scenarios, making amateur radio operators invaluable to disaster relief efforts.

Many hams are members of national and international amateur radio emergency organizations. These organizations put in place protocols that help hams quickly set up radio networks in the event of a disaster. Large relief organizations such as the Red Cross frequently ask these emergency communications organizations for help in areas with no access to the Internet.

Event Coordination

Many major public events utilize amateur radio volunteers to oversee event communications. For example, the Boston Marathon uses hundreds of volunteer amateur radio operators to relay information across the entirety of the course. Figure 7-5 shows a subset of these volunteers. The sheer scale of many events makes other means of communication, such as phone calls, impractical. Hams use a communication structure called a "net" to make relaying information an easier task. Rather than have every operator talk at once, a "net control" coordinates radio traffic to ensure that information gets where it needs to go in a timely fashion. In addition to being efficient, these nets are capable of functioning even if power or Internet connection is lost.

Figure 7-5. *Volunteers at the finish line of the 2019 Boston Marathon, with a few amateur radio volunteers in the mix*

Education

Amateur radio is also a fantastic way to learn more about radio and radio communications. Many amateur radio clubs frequently visit schools to teach young individuals about radio technology. Long-distance contacts are a great way to engage those unfamiliar with radio, so many hams enjoy showing others this capability. Astronauts aboard the International Space Station participate in amateur radio activities and frequently make contacts with schools and educational institutions. Figure 7-6 shows a NASA astronaut operating amateur radio equipment on the International Space Station. As someone learning about radio yourself, I highly recommend exploring amateur radio and seeing what interests you.

Figure 7-6. *NASA astronaut Col. Doug Wheelock operating amateur radio equipment on the International Space Station*

Remote Communications

It's perfectly legal to use amateur radio bands to communicate with robots, satellites, and remote sensors, so oftentimes individuals use them for this purpose. Amateur radio has the advantage of allowing a great deal of customization over off-the-shelf designs. One can modify the output power and frequency of the transmitter to a much greater degree than for unlicensed, commercial transmitters. This certainly isn't necessary for many applications, but for large projects it has its advantages. Amateur radio bands are used very frequently to communicate with small satellites known as "CubeSats," one of which is shown in Figure 7-7.

Figure 7-7. *A CubeSat being launched from the International Space Station. Many CubeSats utilize amateur radio frequencies to send science and telemetry information back to Earth*

Licensing

As briefly mentioned before, one must be licensed in order to transmit on amateur frequencies. This helps ensure that amateur bands stay clean of the pollution that occurs with unlicensed bands such as the 2.4 GHz used for many home devices. Licensed users are much more likely to follow rules about fair use of spectrum, ensuring that amateur bands can be used for the purposes for which they're intended. Having a license also makes you part of a global community of licensed amateur radio operators. All licensed hams are assigned a *callsign* by their licensing body. Callsigns serve as a way to identify others on the air and as a way to prove that you actually are licensed.

This is nice once you're licensed, but it unfortunately means that you'll need to go take a test in a physical location in order to get your license. There are also multiple levels of license that one can have. As your knowledge of radio progresses, you can take tests to unlock additional privileges. The levels of license in the following section are for the United States—many other countries follow a similar format for licensing, but be sure to check online about the details for your country. An example of an FCC amateur radio license is shown in Figure 7-8.

Figure 7-8. *An FCC amateur radio license, with personally identifying information removed*

Technician

Technician license, or "tech," is the lowest level of license one can attain. Passing the technician licensing test is relatively simple, as it requires only a cursory knowledge of radio theory and restrictions imposed by the FCC. Upon obtaining your technician license, the FCC issues you a six-character callsign that allows you to operate on amateur bands above 30 MHz. You do not have full privileges to operate on all these bands as a technician-class licensee—the data transmission format is limited by the FCC.

General

The general test is harder to pass than technician. It has more possible questions about FCC restrictions and asks many more questions relating to operation of lower-frequency bands. A general-class license grants you limited privileges to operate on all amateur bands, although general license holders are still somewhat limited in how information can be transmitted.

Amateur Extra

The extra-class licensing test is harder still to pass, but upon successful completion of the test, you can use all amateur bands with every communications mode allowed by the FCC. Additionally, holding an amateur extra license makes you eligible for the shortest possible callsigns allowed by the FCC.

The Technician Test

Passing the technician licensing exam is by no means assured, but with a little bit of studying on top of the information contained in this book, you should be more than capable of achieving a satisfactory score. The test contains 35 questions, all of which are drawn from a publicly accessible pool of a few hundred questions. It's perfectly feasible to go through all the questions and see the answers ahead of time so you're fully prepared for the test, although this is generally not necessary in order to pass. A passing score for the test is 26 questions correct out of the 35. Getting extra questions correct on top of the 26 will not grant you additional privileges.

In the next section, I've provided some samples to give you a good idea of the type of questions you'll see on the test. I highly recommend additional studying on top of this—there are many questions on FCC restrictions and laws that you will not be able to answer by making an educated guess; you simply have to see the question first. www.HamStudy. org is a fantastic resource for studying, as it has detailed explanations of the answers to most of the questions in the testing pool.

Sample Questions

Don't worry if you don't know the answers—this selection is designed to show you the range of questions on the test. Studying for only a few hours will allow you to answer many of the questions available. The answers to these questions are in the next section.

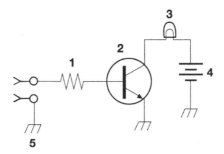

Figure T-1

1. **What is component 2 in Figure T-1?**

    A. Resistor

    B. Transistor

    C. Indicator lamp

    D. Connector

2. **What do the initials LEO tell you about an amateur satellite?**

    A. The satellite battery is in Low Energy Operation mode.

    B. The satellite is in a Low Earth Orbit.

C. The satellite uses Light Emitting Optics.

D. The satellite is performing a Lunar Ejection Orbit maneuver.

3. **In which of the following circumstances may the control operator of an amateur station receive compensation for operating that station?**

   A. When the communication is related to the sale of amateur equipment by the control operator's employer.

   B. When the communication is incidental to classroom instruction at an educational institution.

   C. When the communication is made to obtain emergency information for a local broadcast station.

   D. All of these choices are correct.

4. **What should you do if something in a neighbor's home is causing harmful interference to your amateur station?**

   A. Work with your neighbor to identify the offending device.

   B. Politely inform your neighbor about the rules that prohibit the use of devices that cause interference.

   C. Check your station and make sure it meets the standards of good amateur practice.

   D. All of these choices are correct.

5. **What should be done when using voice modes to ensure that voice messages containing unusual words are received correctly?**

   A. Send the words by voice and Morse code.

   B. Speak very loudly into the microphone.

C. Spell the words using a standard phonetic alphabet.

D. All of these choices are correct.

6. **What is the voltage across each of two components in series with a voltage source?**

A. The same voltage as the source.

B. Half the source voltage.

C. It is determined by the type and value of the components.

D. Twice the source voltage.

7. **Which of the following describes the Radio Amateur Civil Emergency Service (RACES)?**

A. A radio service using amateur frequencies for emergency management or civil defense communications.

B. A radio service using amateur stations for emergency management or civil defense communications.

C. An emergency service using amateur operators certified by a civil defense organization as being enrolled in that organization.

D. All of these choices are correct.

8. **In which direction does a half-wave dipole antenna radiate the strongest signal?**

A. Equally in all directions

B. Off the ends of the antenna

C. Broadside to the antenna

D. In the direction of the feed line

9. **What kind of hazard might exist in a power supply when it is turned off and disconnected?**

    A. Static electricity could damage the grounding system.

    B. Circulating currents inside the transformer might cause damage.

    C. The fuse might blow if you remove the cover.

    D. You might receive an electric shock from the charge stored in large capacitors.

10. **Which frequency is within the 6 m amateur band?**

    A. 49.00 MHz

    B. 52.525 MHz

    C. 28.50 MHz

    D. 222.15 MHz

Answers

1. **B.** Many of the questions on the test check your knowledge of general electrical engineering concepts. Numerous questions ask you to identify the components in this picture.

2. **B.** Some of the questions test your knowledge of more niche topics in amateur radio such as communications with objects in space. In this case, LEO refers to objects in Low Earth Orbit, which is generally considered to be orbits with a maximum altitude below 2,000 km.

3. **B.** This question demonstrates one of the core purposes of amateur radio: education. Hams are not allowed to receive compensation for their services in amateur radio, but this restriction could be problematic for teachers wishing to educate students about radio and amateur radio. Therefore, exemptions to this rule exist in special circumstances such as this one. The general idea of this question is more important than its content: make sure you understand the purpose of amateur radio and its goals.

4. **D.** Some questions test your knowledge of general operating procedures. This question also happens to be part of a large subset of questions that can be answered with common sense—if all of the answers are very reasonable, and there are no specific laws or rules in question, chances are all of them are correct.

5. **C.** This is another example of a commonsense question. You may not know the exact law, but speaking loudly into the microphone is obviously not correct, which removes **B** and **D. C** is more plausible, and it happens to be correct!

6. **C.** This question tests your knowledge of core electrical engineering concepts. I recommend doing further research into basic electrical engineering principles, as it will help further your knowledge of radio in general. This specific question can be answered with a basic knowledge of Ohm's law and the behavior of components connected in series.

7. **D.** A few questions contain information about amateur radio organizations and emergency capabilities of amateur radio. You'll generally need to see these questions ahead of time or know something about the organization in question to get them correct. All of the answers sound basically the same here, so **D** would be a solid guess if you didn't know.

8. **C.** The technician test also contains questions about radio and antenna theory, which this book can help you answer! Recall the radiation pattern of a dipole antenna: it radiates around the face, which can be described as "broadside."

9. **D.** Safety is important in amateur radio, as you may oftentimes deal with large voltages and currents. Knowing the hazards of electrical components is important to safe operation. For this question, knowing that capacitors store energy would help you choose the correct answer.

10. **B.** This is part of a broad class of questions for which you need to calculate the answer. From the chapter on radio theory, you should be familiar with how frequency and wavelength are related. An easy way to calculate this in your head is to perform all the calculations in units of 1 million. The speed of light is roughly 300 million meters per second, and we're looking for a frequency in megahertz. The frequency of a wave is its speed divided by its wavelength, so $300/6 = 50$ MHz.

Finding a Test

The best way to find a license test center is to simply search "Ham radio license test locations" online. Most medium-size cities have clubs that offer tests on a regular basis, so it shouldn't be too hard to find a place to get licensed. Your test will be administered by VEs, or volunteer examiners. Chatting with your VEs and other individuals before and after the test is a great way to learn more about the hobby and hear others' experiences, so don't be shy! After you take and pass your test, your callsign will appear in your government's database within a few days or weeks. At this point, you're fully licensed to be on the air.

Summary

Amateur radio is a versatile hobby that allows you to contact others in interesting ways while learning about radio in the process. Amateur radio operators, or "hams," utilize specially allocated regions of the electromagnetic spectrum for their communications. These regions are usually dedicated only to amateur radio, but are sometimes shared for military or other purposes. Regardless of your country of residence, you will need to acquire a license to transmit on amateur radio frequencies. One can obtain a license through a licensing test, generally administered by the body of your government responsible for regulating communications.

A key restriction of transmissions on amateur radio frequencies is that they cannot be commercial in nature. Opening up amateur frequencies to commercial activity would render them useless for the purposes of amateur radio. These purposes include civil emergency communications, education, event coordination, general communications, and more. In the next chapter, you'll learn how to operate amateur radio equipment and contact others.

CHAPTER 8

Handheld Transceivers and Repeaters

This chapter is meant to introduce you to some of the technology that powers the world of amateur radio. We'll first cover the handheld transceiver (HT), a small radio that allows you to get on the air quickly. Even if you don't have your license, you can still participate in this chapter. Just know that you cannot transmit anything until you're licensed.

Your Handheld Transceiver

The handheld transceiver we'll be using throughout this book is the BaoFeng UV-5R (shown in Figure 8-1). There are many variants of this radio, and they all have basically the same features. BaoFeng is a Chinese company that was the first to really introduce low-cost HTs to the masses. These are oftentimes the first radios that a ham will purchase, and they usually work for years without any problems. Low-cost BaoFeng radios are by no means perfect, but they're a great way to get on the air for new hams. They feature comparable specifications to mid-range transceivers that cost $100+. If you haven't picked one up yet, go to the "Materials" section of this

© Alex Wulff 2019
A. Wulff, *Beginning Radio Communications*,
https://doi.org/10.1007/978-1-4842-5302-1_8

book and buy one from the link provided. If you already have a different handheld transceiver, you should still be able to follow along.

Figure 8-1. *The BaoFeng BF-F8+, which is almost identical to the UV-5R. Other similar variants of this radio look exactly the same, except for the text at the bottom of the radio indicating the model*

A common criticism of these radios is that they enable unlicensed individuals to utilize amateur radio frequencies, as the radios are cheap and somewhat easy to use. It's not uncommon for groups of individuals to pick up a set of these radios and use them to communicate while hiking, skiing, and more. But this is *illegal*. If you do not have proper licensing, you cannot use the transmit functionality of these radios (or any that utilize amateur frequencies). It is perfectly legal, however, to listen to whatever you want using your HT without a license. If you haven't taken the licensing test yet, you can still participate in the exercises in this chapter by listening instead of both transmitting and listening.

You could be forgiven for confusing your HT with a generic walkie-talkie such as the ones in Figure 8-2. At their cores, both devices have a very similar function: transmit/receive voice information over radio waves. Where walkie-talkies use opaquely defined "channels" to obscure the real transmit/receive frequency, HTs allow the user to directly set the transmit and receive frequency to within 5 kHz steps. Most walkie-talkies operate in a special portion of the 2 m band reserved for walkie-talkies, while your HT can transmit and receive on amateur radio 2 m and 70 cm bands.

Figure 8-2. *A selection of walkie-talkies, each of which looks very similar to a typical handheld transceiver*

Another difference is transmit power. Most walkie-talkies output around 0.5 W or 1 W, which allows for communications at a maximum of a few miles. Your BaoFeng UV-5R can output up to 5 W, increasing the maximum range to a few tens of miles with a good antenna. In proper conditions, individuals have made contacts using 5 W and the stock antenna from over 100 miles away. This is most often only possible from high elevations free of obstructions in the path.

Another cool feature of HTs is your ability to use them with all kinds of antennas. Walkie-talkies have an antenna attached to the device, but all HTs offer an interconnect that allows you to disconnect the stock antenna and attach whatever you want. The stock antenna on BaoFengs is notoriously bad, so many opt to purchase better-matched "rubber ducky" antennas of the same form factor. You can also use an HT with a more elaborate antenna setup, such as the optional log-periodic antenna in the "Materials" section. This enables extremely long-distance contacts such as with satellites. A handheld transceiver with a special rollable antenna is shown in Figure 8-3. Lastly, HTs have many software-configurable features that make them useful to hams. We will explore many of these in the following sections!

Figure 8-3. *A handheld transceiver connected to a "slim jim" antenna. These antennas can be rolled up when not in use, and provide much better gain at VHF and UHF than the stock antenna*

Using Your Handheld Transceiver

The first thing you should do when you get your radio is place it in its provided charging cradle. The radio and cradle are shown in Figure 8-4. The battery life on these devices is quite good; with infrequent transmissions, you can expect it to last for an entire day. Keep it charging until the light on the front of the cradle turns green, which indicates that it's done charging.

Figure 8-4. *A BaoFeng UV-5R in its charging cradle*

Next, remove your radio from the charging cradle and turn it on by twisting the knob at the top. In addition to powering on/off the radio, this knob controls the output volume of the speaker. Your radio should greet you with a series of beeps, and the display should light up. We'll first start by identifying all the buttons on the radio and their function.

- Pressing the red button on the left side (labelled "call") will switch the radio to FM-radio-receive mode. Any incoming signals on the amateur frequency the radio is set to will automatically silence the FM radio. Holding the call button will activate alarm mode, which you should avoid doing.

- The button below call is PTT, or push-to-talk. This will activate the transmit function of the radio and transmit your voice! If you're unlicensed, pressing this button is illegal.

- The button below PTT is used to turn on the flashlight or open the squelch (discussed later).

- Next, looking at the face of the radio you should see a button labelled "VFO/MR." This allows you to configure your radio between stored channel mode and frequency mode. In frequency mode, you can manually set the transmit and receive frequency of the radio. In channel mode, you can cycle between preprogrammed channels.

- The "A/B" button allows you to switch between the frequencies or channels on the upper and lower portions of the display.

- The "menu" button allows you to configure the settings of your radio. In the menu screen, you can cycle between different options by pressing the up and down arrow keys, or you can type the number of a given option to access it quickly. Once you've reached the desired setting, you can access it by again pressing the menu button, and then you can change the setting with the number keys or arrow keys. Pressing the menu button again will save your selection—you need to do this after you change any setting, as they do not save automatically. You can press the "exit" button to return to normal operation.

- While in frequency mode, you can enter the frequency at which you wish to transmit and receive through the number keys. In channel mode, entering a number with the number keys will take you to that channel.

Don't worry if the interface seems confusing at first—it is confusing, but you'll learn it quickly if you use your radio frequently. Table 8-1 lists some common menu options that you'll likely need to use at some point.

Table 8-1. Useful BaoFeng menu options.

Number	Name	Description
0	SQL	"Squelch" is essentially a threshold that the received signal must surpass in order to be output to the speaker. This saves you from constantly hearing noise.
2	TXP	This setting is the transmit power. You can change this between LOW (1 W) or HIGH (5 W).
13	T-CTCS	Transmit-continuous tone coded squelch is explained more in the following, but you'll likely need to modify this in order to communicate through repeaters.
25	SFT-D	Shift direction. Again, this is explained in the following, but you will likely need to modify this setting at some point.
26	OFFSET	This is another setting that you'll need to communicate with repeaters which is also explained in the following.
40	RESET	If you mess something up, you can quickly reset your radio with this option.

Repeaters

Now that you're familiar with how your radio operates, you can use it to do interesting things! An integral part of HT-based amateur radio communications is *repeaters*. Repeaters are devices that accept incoming voice signals and rebroadcast them at a much higher power at a slightly different frequency. This enables a simple handheld transceiver to communicate with devices across a large swath of area, generally many tens of miles in diameter. The repeater may not provide much benefit for transmissions close to you, but it can effectively double the maximum range of transmissions to distant handheld transceivers. Even if your device cannot reach a given receiver, you can often still hear transmissions from it. Some repeaters have coverage maps that show the maximum distance from which an individual can typically hear transmissions. Figure 8-5 is an example of a coverage map. This map does not show the coverage of a repeater, but rather a weather radio station operated by NOAA. This station transmits at 1 kW, and is located in New York City. Coverage maps are generally computer simulated based on the geography of the region.

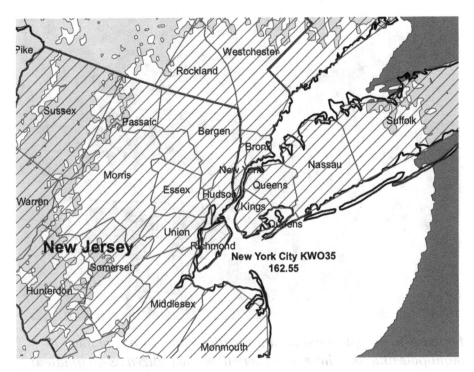

Figure 8-5. *A typical coverage map, with coverage shown in white*

Repeaters are most often tower-based devices. The actual signal processing hardware is quite compact, but to get a decent amount of coverage, one must mount antennas for the system atop a tower. Repeaters can be placed on mountaintops or hills, and share the same tower as other communications equipment (see Figure 8-6). Repeaters are managed by individuals or amateur radio clubs in that region.

Figure 8-6. *A typical telecommunications tower—one of the monopole antennas here could very likely be utilized as an amateur radio repeater*

Your HT is well equipped to communicate with repeaters. There are plenty of 70 cm and 2 m repeaters, both of which you can transmit to and receive from using your HT. You generally need to know three things to communicate with a repeater: frequency, offset, and private line (PL) tone.

Repeater Frequency

The listed frequency for a repeater is the frequency at which the repeater transmits signals. If you just want to listen to transmissions from the repeater, you can simply tune your radio to this frequency and be done. If you want to transmit through a repeater, you'll need more information. As mentioned before, repeaters transmit at a different frequency than they receive. This helps prevent interference from many hams trying to talk at the same time.

Repeater Offset

The repeater offset is the distance, in frequency, between the transmit frequency and the receive frequency. Almost all 2 m repeaters utilize a 600 kHz offset, and almost all 70 cm repeaters utilize a 5 MHz offset. You need to know the *offset direction* for a given repeater, which describes the direction in which the offset is applied. For example, a repeater operating at 147.000 MHz (which is in the 2 m band) with a positive offset will transmit signals at 147.000 MHz and accept incoming signals at 147.600 MHz.

Repeaters are generally listed something like "147.000+"—the frequency of the repeater is the number, and then the offset direction is either a "+" or a "-" to indicate a positive or negative offset. You can set the offset direction in your radio by going to menu setting 25, which is also listed in Table 8-1. When active, a plus or a minus sign will appear on your display, and when transmitting the displayed frequency will change to the base frequency plus or minus the offset. This is shown in Figure 8-7. Ensure that you know when this setting is operational, as it can cause transmissions to something other than a repeater to fail if the receiving device is not configured to use an offset.

Figure 8-7. *The screen of an HT when a positive offset is applied. Notice the "+" located at the top*

PL Tone

Most repeaters will not accept incoming transmissions that are not accompanied by a special subaudible tone. This is mainly to prevent unintended activation of the repeater by noise or spurious signals. This tone is often called a PL ("private line") tone or a CTCSS ("continuous tone-coded squelch system") tone. These are the same thing. As described before, squelch is a way to prevent your radio from constantly being activated by noise. CTCSS is merely a smarter way to activate a repeater or a radio. Repeaters have specific PL tones that will activate them, and they will not activate if they don't receive this specific tone.

PL tones are generally in the range of 50 Hz–150 Hz, which are considered to be subaudible. PL tones are configurable in your radio using menu option 13. A full listing for a repeater will generally appear as "147.000+ PL 71.9." You already know what the first part of this indicates, and the number after "PL" indicates the PL tone (measured in Hz). Leaving the PL tone on for transmissions other than to a device configured to use them is harmless. The tone is subaudible, so the receiving device will not even notice that it's there unless specifically designed to listen for a PL tone. Much like with offsets, your HT will indicate if a PL tone is active. The tone screen is shown in Figure 8-8, and some radios indicate that a tone is active on the main screen.

Figure 8-8. *The PL tone menu screen*

Finding a Repeater

You now know the basics of how repeaters operate, but how can you actually obtain information about repeaters in your area? As usual, the answer is the Internet. Searching "amateur radio repeaters in ____," with the line replaced with the name of the closest city to you, will generally provide a comprehensive list. You'll be surprised at just how many repeaters there are in your area—there's a large community of hams all across the globe that dedicate a significant amount of time building repeater networks. You can also purchase a book called a *Repeater Directory* which lists repeaters by city or state.

Some repeaters form a linked network. Signals picked up by one repeater will be broadcast by all other repeaters linked to it, allowing for extremely long-distance communications. The fact that a repeater is linked to another is normally indicated in the repeater listing. You'll generally find that you can reach repeaters a maximum of 15 miles away with 5 W, or the highest transmit power of your radio. A general rule of thumb is if you can see a repeater, you can probably reach it.

Some repeaters are part of the EchoLink system—EchoLink allows you to connect to any repeater that's a part of its system via the Internet. You can both monitor transmissions coming into the repeater and send your voice out over the repeater with no radio required. EchoLink is a great way to monitor repeaters if you don't have a radio on you, but you'll need to have an FCC callsign to sign up. Repeaters that are part of the EchoLink system are given a node ID that you can utilize to connect to them.

Making a Repeater Contact

Hams operating other voice modes and bands than FM and VHF/UHF oftentimes utilize *calling frequencies* to initiate a contact. A calling frequency is a predetermined frequency where one would advertise a desire to initiate a contact. Since these other bands propagate farther and are usually operated with higher-power equipment, it's easy to find a contact this way—however, this is unsuitable for handheld transceivers, as they operate across a very limited geographical range.

Local amateur radio operators with HTs will instead rely on repeaters as common frequencies at which to make a contact. Many individuals leave their radios on and constantly tuned to repeater frequencies to pick up such contacts if they occur. If you're lucky, someone is listening to a repeater around you right now!

Due to repeaters' function as local "gathering places" for hams, many new hams make their first contacts through a repeater. Unless you're in a densely populated area, you may never find hams talking on frequencies other than those used by a repeater with your handheld transceiver. Repeaters have the added benefit of being geographically optimized for an area. In a valley, transmissions will generally be blocked by the hills or mountains on either side. Repeaters at the top of the hill can rebroadcast your signal out of the valley and across the surrounding area.

Let's now set up your radio. Configure your radio with the correct frequency, offset, and PL tone for a repeater around you. Once you think everything is set up correctly, you're ready to go! To initiate contact on a repeater, one usually says his/her callsign followed by the word "listening." This indicates to other hams that may be on the repeater that you are monitoring the repeater and looking for a contact. Before doing this, ensure that the repeater is not currently in use by listening for a minute. If a conversation is currently underway, you can break in by announcing your callsign and your name in the gap between exchanges.

Many repeaters are configured with a courtesy tone to show you that your transmissions are going through and to indicate that the last ham that transmitted has released the repeater and someone else can transmit. After announcing your callsign and "listening," your radio should light up for a few seconds after your transmission with a signal and possibly a short tone coming back from the repeater. If nothing happens after you release the transmit button, it's entirely possible that you have configured your settings incorrectly (or you're out of range of a repeater). All repeaters I've seen will at least have a few seconds of silent signal after a transmission.

For your first few contacts, it's also important to indicate to the other ham that you're new to the hobby. You'll likely make mistakes, and hopefully the other ham will identify these mistakes for you and help you correct them. Almost all hams love teaching and informing others, so don't hesitate to ask for help or clarifications when necessary.

If you don't hear anything back, but you know your transmission is going through, try repeating your callsign followed by "listening" every minute for a few minutes until you get something, or switch to a different repeater. It's also a good idea to leave your radio on and tuned to the frequency of a repeater in your area. Sooner or later, you're bound to hear someone. You're more likely to get a contact on a repeater that's linked to other repeaters, as this system inevitably covers a larger geographic area.

If you're having trouble hitting repeaters around you, try utilizing your log-periodic antenna. This requires that you know the location of a given repeater—you need to point your antenna at the repeater in order for it to be effective. You may also need to twist the antenna such that the radiating elements are vertical, as repeaters' antennas are generally vertically polarized. This is shown in Figure 8-9. Note how the antenna in the figure is twisted so that the elements are vertically polarized. High-gain antennas such as this can be utilized to reach repeaters with obstacles in the way, such as the trees shown in the figure. Instructions on how to use this antenna are located in the following chapter.

Figure 8-9. *Using a log-periodic antenna for repeater contacts*

Summary

Congratulations! You now know how to operate your first piece of amateur radio hardware! With your handheld transceiver, the BaoFeng UV-5R, you can use repeaters to contact individuals many miles away. Repeaters will be your gateway to the amateur radio community until you invest in fixed hardware that allows for longer-distance operation. Repeaters are convenient ways to talk with others; additionally, they serve as common gathering places for hams to talk with one another.

Clearly, handheld transceivers are versatile devices that open the door to the world of amateur radio. Many hams don't purchase other radio equipment than handheld transceivers for years after they get their license as these devices are so capable. It's well worth it to spend your time getting to know your handheld transceiver, as it will become an invaluable tool in your radio toolbox. BaoFeng radios do have shortcomings, particularly in their voice quality and receiver hardware. If you enjoy amateur radio, it might be a good idea to invest in a more expensive HT—you can find decent used models in the range of $100 or $200. In the next chapter, we will use an HT and a specialized antenna to communicate with other hams via a satellite.

CHAPTER 9

Amateur Radio Satellites

One of the downsides of your HT is its limited geographic reach, even with accompanying repeaters. Believe it or not, it's actually possible to reach individuals thousands of miles away utilizing your HT and a more advanced antenna. This setup is shown in Figure 9-1. The only caveat here is that you'll be relaying your communications directly through an amateur radio satellite. Until you set up your own amateur radio shack with a fixed antenna, communications through a satellite will likely be your only means of cross-continental communications.

© Alex Wulff 2019
A. Wulff, *Beginning Radio Communications*,
https://doi.org/10.1007/978-1-4842-5302-1_9

Figure 9-1. *The author working an amateur radio satellite*

The equipment shown here is a five-element log-periodic antenna (connected to a software-defined radio) for receiving transmissions and an HT for sending transmissions.

Ham Satellite Overview

You can think of amateur radio satellites as repeaters orbiting the Earth. They function in almost exactly the same way as a repeater, with different transmit and receive frequencies and PL tones. The only main technical differences between ham satellites and repeaters are transmit power and split operation. These satellites oftentimes have very small solar panels to provide power, so consequently their transmit power is extremely low (usually much less than 1 W). This means that even trees between you and the sky can severely diminish signal quality. Additionally, these satellites utilize different bands for transmitting and receiving—many use VHF as an uplink and UHF as a downlink. This "split operation" *is* possible with your HT, but it requires that you utilize a computer to program in the information for a given satellite.

The other difficult aspect of communications with amateur radio satellites is the fact that they're in orbit. Much like with the weather satellites we explored previously, you'll only have a small window a few times a day that you can receive signals from them. We will also be using a directional antenna to do this, so you'll need to track the satellite across the sky with the antenna and operate the radio at the same time. This antenna is shown in Figure 9-2. Although the task of tracking appears daunting, it can become quite easy with practice, and making a contact in a different part of your country with limited equipment can be a satisfying feeling.

Figure 9-2. *The antenna used in this chapter: an Elk Antennas five-element dualband log-periodic antenna*

The reason for the special antenna is the increased directional gain that it provides. A directional antenna will, depending upon the type, allow for around an 8 dB increase in signal reception over the antenna on your HT. This can mean the difference between hearing just static at the output of your HT and hearing clear voice transmissions. The particular antenna used for this project, a log-periodic, does not provide as much forward gain as a typical Yagi. A log-periodic is necessary because they are more well suited to operate at both VHF and UHF, at the expense of directionality.

If you opted not to purchase the log-periodic antenna, it's still certainly possible to participate in this exercise. You can hear transmissions from various amateur radio satellites with nothing but your HT and its stock antenna; however, the satellite needs to be relatively high in the sky, decreasing the available window of operation. It's also somewhat challenging to correctly orient the monopole antenna on your HT such that the polarization and gain pattern is always optimal. Signals on the ground are generally polarized vertically, but most satellites transmit in a horizontally polarized configuration. Some also tumble in orbit, causing the signal to fade in and out with a constant period as the polarization changes.

If you do opt to just utilize your HT, you should orient your HT's antenna parallel to the ground and in a direction that's perpendicular to the path of the satellite. Such a configuration is shown in Figure 9-3. You should also only expect to hear transmissions with the satellite relatively high in the sky.

Figure 9-3. *How to correctly orient the rubber ducky antenna on your HT to receive satellite transmissions*

The trajectory of the satellite in the sky is shown in red. This means orienting the antenna is only a rule of thumb—you should always try twisting your antenna in different configurations to see what gives you the best signal.

CHIRP

CHIRP is a free and open-source software tool that you can use to program your HT. Its logo is shown in Figure 9-4. You'd go crazy attempting to manually program the information of satellites/repeaters every time you want to try one, so CHIRP is a valuable tool to learn. You can create different programming profiles for different purposes, as well. For example, many volunteer events send out lists of the frequencies, PL tones, and offsets used for that event that you can import into CHIRP and program your radio with. Such events almost never directly refer to frequencies and instead use channel names that also get programmed and displayed on your radio. After such an event, I'll switch back to my custom list of repeaters by simply reprogramming my radio with a different list.

Figure 9-4. *The logo of CHIRP, the software we'll use to program the BaoFeng UV-5R*

In order to use CHIRP, you'll need the programming cable for your radio that was mentioned in the "Materials" section. This cable takes information from your computer via USB and translates it into a digital audio format that your radio expects. I've found that the programming and operation aspects of CHIRP are normally not the difficult part; instead, it can sometimes be a challenge to get all the necessary drivers installed and get your cable communicating correctly with your radio.

Acquiring Satellite Frequencies

CHIRP isn't much use if you don't have any frequencies to program. The first step is identifying the information of active amateur radio satellites. I have only successfully made contacts through a handful of satellites, but theoretically there are many in operation. These satellites are not launched or funded by governments; instead, amateur radio organizations develop these satellites and pay for the launches themselves. Launching and developing large satellites is prohibitively expensive, so amateur radio satellites are generally tiny (hence the limited transmit power). Many use the standardized CubeSat form to save money. CubeSats, as you can likely guess, are cubes. Each side measures 10 cm.

I have compiled a list of satellites that I know are operational and easy to access—you can find the list at www.AlexWulff.com/RadioBook/ SatList. In this list, you'll find the names of the satellites, their associated frequencies, PL tones, tracking information, and notes. A screenshot of this web site is shown in Figure 9-5.

Name	Uplink	Downlink	PL Tone	Tracking	Notes
SO-50	145.850	436.795	67.0	Link Passes	Needs to be armed with PL tone of 74.4 Hz before use (if not active).
AO-91	435.250	145.960	67.0	Link Passes	
AO-92	435.350	145.880	67.0	Link Passes	Sometimes operates with a 1.2 GHz uplink.
CHIRP Config					Use this file with CHIRP to upload these satellites to your HT. If your radio model is different than the one in the file you can copy and paste the fields to a config file for your radio.
GoSatWatch					My favorite iOS satellite tracking application.

Figure 9-5. *The satellite list, with additional files*

I highly recommend searching online to find additional satellites that you want to try. Also on this page is a link to download a configuration file that you can use to program your radio via CHIRP. This profile allows you to skip the following steps of entering the satellite information. I will discuss how to use this later, but first I think it's important to outline the process of loading in the satellite information manually via CHIRP. You'll inevitably have to program your HT, so it's critical to learn how to perform this task.

Programming via CHIRP

You can start by downloading CHIRP. The installer for your platform is here: https://chirp.danplanet.com/projects/chirp/wiki/Download. Depending upon your platform, you may also need to download and install an accompanying runtime. See the preceding link for instructions. Additionally, you may need to download and install drivers for the cable. The cable listed in the "Materials" section is a genuine programming cable from BaoFeng; as such, you can install genuine FTDI drivers available here: www.ftdichip.com/Drivers/VCP.htm. Knock-off programming cables require drivers that are difficult to find, so it's well worth your money to purchase a genuine cable.

Next, open up CHIRP, and you should be presented with a blank screen. CHIRP can be utilized to program a variety of radios, each of which uses a different format for channel information. The easiest way to ensure that CHIRP is configured correctly is by downloading the initial configuration profile from your radio and then editing and reprogramming it back into your radio. The steps to do this are as follows:

1. Start by clicking the "Radio" menu option and then "Download From Radio." This will load the profile that comes preprogrammed into your radio into CHIRP.

2. You can then select the proper port. Your computer should recognize the FTDI chip in your programming cable, and it should appear in this list if the driver is configured correctly. If you're not sure which device the programming cable is, you can try the following steps multiple times and select a different port each time until it works.

3. Select "BaoFeng" as the vendor, and for the model select whatever it says on the bottom of the front face of your radio. If you get a message about how the radio selection is incorrect, or if your radio is not in the list, then try selecting "UV-5R."

4. Select "OK," and follow the instructions that CHIRP provides. If all goes well, your radio's lights will flash as it transfers over its channel list. This list will then appear in CHIRP, as shown in Figure 9-6.

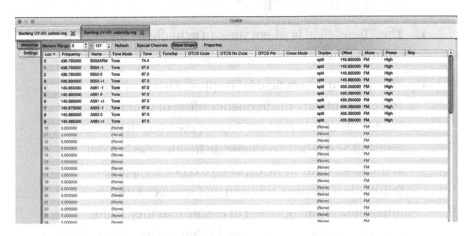

Figure 9-6. *A channel list in CHIRP*

Let's now go over what some of the listed fields do:

- "Loc" is the channel number. On your radio, you can go to a specific channel by entering the channel's number on the keypad while in channel mode.

- "Frequency" is the receive frequency of a given channel. From your work with repeaters, you know that the transmit frequency can be different based on the configuration of the radio.

- "Name" is a short string of text that will appear on your radio's display when tuned to a specific channel. This makes it much easier to identify a channel instead of memorizing what each channel number is.

- "Tone Mode" allows you to configure the subaudible tones that your radio is capable of emitting during a transmission. The "Tone" selection in this list is equivalent to CTCSS or PL tone, while other options can be utilized in different systems. I've never used anything other than "Tone."

- The "Tone" field is where you can actually set the emitted tone.

- The next important field is "Duplex." This is where you can configure the frequency offset of your radio. Your HT is capable of half-duplex, meaning that it can transmit and receive on separate frequencies but not at the same time. More expensive HTs are capable of full-duplex: they can transmit and receive at the same time, allowing an operator to ensure that they're not talking over another individual's signal. The "+" and "-" options are the positive and negative offset that you're already familiar with. "Split" mode utilizes separate bands for transmit and receive.

Programming Satellite Frequencies

Most listings of a given amateur radio satellite, including my own that's linked above, will contain three things: an uplink frequency, a downlink frequency, and a PL tone. The uplink frequency is the frequency at which one must transmit in order to have a signal rebroadcast by the satellite. The downlink frequency is the frequency at which one listens to hear communications coming from the satellite. Finally, the PL tone is the tone necessary to activate the satellite's receiver. An example listing is shown in Figure 9-7.

Name	Uplink	Downlink	PL Tone
SO-50	145.850	436.795	67.0

Figure 9-7. An example listing for SO-50. The uplink and downlink frequencies are in MHz, and the PL tone is in Hz

You might imagine that we'll devote one channel to each satellite, but it's actually helpful to have three. As the satellite moves toward and away from you, its motion will induce a significant Doppler shift. Satellites in low Earth orbit move, relative to the ground, at around 8 km per second. This induces a Doppler shift of a few kilohertz for ground-based radios. Programming in channels with a receive frequency that's 5 kHz above and below the listed frequency will allow you to have better reception as the satellite comes into view and as the satellite fades from view.

One would use the slightly higher receive frequency as the satellite is low on the horizon and gaining in elevation, the normal receive frequency as the satellite is relatively high in the sky, and finally the lowest receive frequency as the satellite recedes from view. With the satellite low in the sky and gaining in elevation, the satellite is moving toward the observer, creating a positive Doppler shift. As the satellite is high in the sky, it's moving transverse to the observer, inducing no Doppler shift. As the satellite is lower in the sky and losing elevation, its motion induces a negative Doppler shift, as it's moving away from the observer.

With all the setup out of the way, we can get programming! I'll show you how to program the information for one satellite, but the procedure is exactly the same for other satellites. The satellite we'll load in is Saudisat

SO-50, a very active and popular satellite among amateur radio satellite enthusiasts. It has a downlink frequency of 436.795 MHz, an uplink frequency of 145.850 MHz, and a PL tone of 67 Hz. This particular satellite also has a timer that needs to be armed if no one has transmitted on the satellite for 10 minutes; we'll program a channel that arms the timer, but this feature is not found on all satellites.

1. Select a group of four adjacent channels. For simplicity, we'll be using channels zero, one, two, and three.

2. We'll set channel zero as the timer-arm channel. If you don't hear anything on the satellite, you can set SO-50's timer by transmitting this channel for a few seconds and then attempt to make a voice contact. Under "Frequency," put 436.795.

3. Name it something like "SO50ARM" to indicate that this is the timer-arm channel. The display on your radio can only fit very short strings of text.

4. Select "Tone" under "Tone Mode," and under the "Tone" field put 74.4. This tone will arm SO-50's timer.

5. Set "Duplex" to "split."

6. The "Offset" frequency should be the uplink frequency, which is 145.850 (MHz). If "Duplex" is set to split, then this field is used as the transmit frequency. Otherwise, this field is added or subtracted from the "Frequency" field to get the transmit frequency, such as with repeater offsets.

    • Ensure that "Mode" is "FM" and "Power" is "High." Figures 9-8 and 9-9 show the setup in CHIRP as described above.

Loc ▼	Frequency	Name	Tone Mode	Tone
0	436.795000	S050ARM	Tone	74.4
1	436.790000	S050 -1	Tone	67.0
2	436.795000	S050 0	Tone	67.0
3	436.800000	S050 +1	Tone	67.0

Figure 9-8. *The Loc, Frequency, Name, Tone Mode, and Tone fields for SO-50 as shown in CHIRP*

Duplex	Offset	Mode	Power
split	145.850000	FM	High
split	145.850000	FM	High
split	145.850000	FM	High
split	145.850000	FM	High

Figure 9-9. *The Duplex, Offset, Mode, and Power fields for SO-50 as shown in CHIRP*

You can then program channels one through three in a similar fashion for the actual channels that you'll use to communicate with SO-50. Increase the receive frequency by 5 kHz in each subsequent channel, starting at 436.790 MHz and ending at 436.800 MHz. The PL tone should also be changed to 67 Hz, as the PL tone will be different from the timer-arm tone. Name each channel something that allows you to determine which has the negative Doppler shift, zero Doppler shift, or positive Doppler shift. If you're confused, the preceding figures show all the described fields and options. You can repeat this procedure for all other satellites with which you may wish to communicate.

Hardware Preparations

The antenna listed in the "Materials" section of Chapter 1 will require some basic setup. Instructions for this are included in the box, which you should follow and complete. This particular log-periodic from Elk Antennas is a favorite of mine as the setup is very simple and the finished antenna is somewhat compact. For storage, you can unscrew the antenna elements and slip the entire thing back into the box. Ensure that you place the colored elements in their proper places, or your antenna will not work correctly. The disassembled antenna is shown in Figure 9-10.

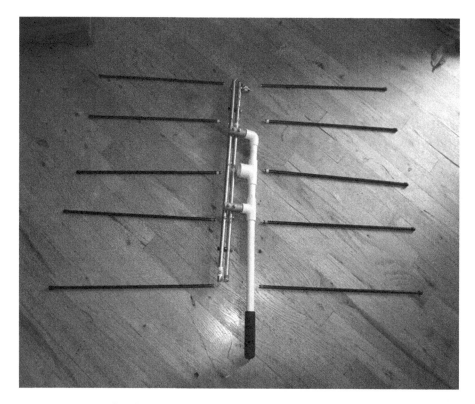

Figure 9-10. *The dissasembled log-periodic atenna*

Connecting the antenna to your radio requires a few adapters and a cable. The antenna is equipped with a "UHF" connector—the name of this connector is very confusing, as it can be used for RF signals of any frequency, not just UHF. Connect the UHF to the SMA adapter listed in the "Materials" section on the antenna. Next, unscrew the antenna on your HT. Your HT utilizes an SMA male connector—to connect it to the antenna, first screw in the SMA female to SMA female adapter and then use the SMA cable to connect the HT to the log-periodic antenna. If you're confused, a diagram showing the connections is shown in Figure 9-11.

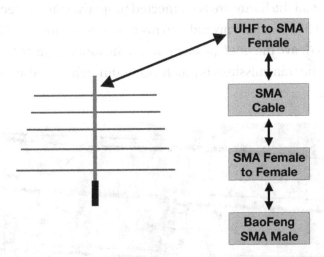

Figure 9-11. *A flowchart depicting the adapter connections between your HT and the log-periodic antenna*

An important aspect of operating radio equipment is ensuring proper connections between items in your setup. With just the HT and its antenna, it's pretty easy to ensure a snug connection. However, as the number of connections increases (such as in the current setup), a loose connector can go unnoticed for a while. Loose connectors can severely degrade signal quality and leak RF energy that can cause harmful interference. The best way to ensure a good connection is to use a wrench, but if you don't have one that will fit around the SMA connectors, then the best thing you can do is periodically tighten the connectors with your fingers.

A good way to observe the degradation of signal quality is to simply unscrew the monopole that came with your HT as you listen to a signal. Furthermore, transmitting with a loose connector will damage your radio. If the connection to the antenna is not tight, energy will be reflected back into your radio's circuitry and damage it. You should never try and transmit without an attached antenna for this reason.

Now that all the hardware is connected properly, you can secure everything. I like to attach my radio to my antenna as shown in Figure 9-12. It's helpful to leave the mic/speaker port on the radio unobstructed— listening to the transmissions is much easier through a headset instead of the speaker.

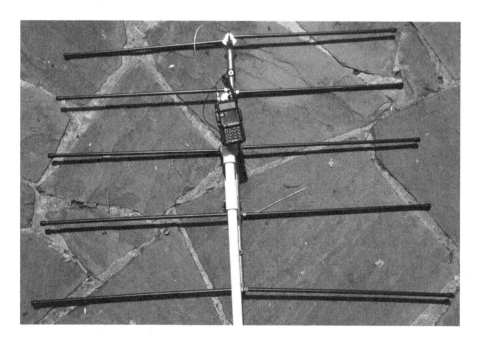

Figure 9-12. The HT fully connected to the antenna

Satellite Tracking

Tracking amateur radio satellites is quite easy with the plethora of online satellite tracking tools available. On my satellite list at `www.AlexWulff.com/RadioBook/SatList`, you can find links to tracking information and pass predictions for each of the listed satellites. As with the weather satellites, a pass is characterized by its maximum elevation. You'll have the most success with passes that have a maximum elevation in excess of 50 degrees. Unlike with the weather satellites, you'll need to know where the amateur radio satellite is at all times during the pass so you can point your antenna at it.

You can do this manually by determining where the satellite rises above the horizon and where it sets and using the duration of the pass to estimate where the satellite will be, but a mobile application will vastly simplify things. Mobile satellite tracking apps show you exactly where a satellite is in the sky on your phone or tablet, taking the guess work out of pointing the antenna. Some apps are listed at the linked web site with the list of satellites. My favorite, GoSatWatch, is shown in Figure 9-13. I recommend testing whichever app you select beforehand on a different satellite, so you're not fumbling around with it during a pass.

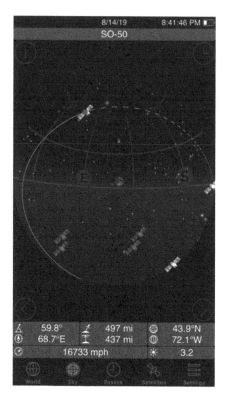

Figure 9-13. *GoSatWatch's sky view, with the trajectory of an SO-50 pass shown*

Working a Satellite

Once you've selected a satellite, programmed in the proper frequencies, identified a viable pass, and set up your hardware, you're ready to go! Before attempting to transmit and communicate, I recommend practicing by listening to a few passes. This will give you experience with following the satellite across the sky and ensuring that your equipment is functioning properly. Figure 9-14 shows me working AO-92.

Figure 9-14.   *The author working AO-92*

The beamwidth of the log-periodic antenna is relatively wide, so you only need to point it in the general direction of the satellite. You can find the satellite by sweeping the antenna across the sky. Some satellites tumble in orbit, so their antenna polarization is not always horizontal. In this case, rotating the antenna slightly gave the best signal quality.

You should find a relatively open area such as a large field in which to work the satellite. Objects that obstruct your view of the sky will also block the weak signals coming from the satellite. Start by setting the squelch on your HT to zero, such that noise starts coming out of your radio. The signal may not be strong enough to trigger the squelch during a pass, which is why it's good to set the squelch to zero. As the pass starts, point your antenna where you think the satellite is. The shorter elements are toward the front of the antenna—it's important that you get the orientation correct. Mixing up the front and back is easy to do, and results in a huge degradation of signal quality.

If everything is programmed correctly and the satellite is active, you should eventually hear individuals' voices coming in through the noise. I've found that I can start to hear transmissions once the satellite gets about 15–20 degrees above the horizon. Start with the channel that you programmed with a negative Doppler shift, and occasionally cycle between different Doppler shifts (positive, negative, or zero) to see what gives you the best reception.

Some satellites' transmissions are not polarized horizontally. During a pass, you should also try twisting the antenna (by rotating your arm) to see what orientation gives the clearest reception. This also serves as a great demonstration of the extent to which polarization can affect received signal strength. A clear transmission polarized in one direction can be almost unintelligible if the receiving antenna is polarized perpendicularly.

What You'll Hear

Particularly active satellites can sound quite hectic; since these repeaters cover such a broad area, sometimes there can be literally hundreds of people all attempting to work a satellite at once. Most transmissions contain two key things: a callsign and a *grid square*. A callsign is mandated for any transmission on amateur radio bands, and it also serves as a convenient way to later look up whom you just made contact with. Many individuals will record the callsigns of others during a contact and log them later.

A *grid square* is a string of letters and numbers that specifies a particular location on the globe. Grid squares are comprised of a four-character grid square and a two-character suffix. The four-character grid square specifies a rectangle a few hundred miles on each side, and the suffix identifies an area within that grid square that's a few miles by a few miles. Web sites such as www.qrz.com/gridmapper allow you to identify your own square and look up the squares of others.

There isn't much of a use for grid squares when communicating through repeaters, as every individual is generally in the same area. However, with long-distance communications such as through a satellite, grid squares allow you to pinpoint the location of the contacts. A typical voice contact through a satellite will begin with the individual's callsign, followed by the grid square. It will sound something like "This is KD2ZZZ from FN13" (the letters are oftentimes spoken phonetically to improve clarity). Another individual might then affirm the contact and reply with his/her callsign and grid square. Unless the satellite is relatively inactive, little contact other than callsign and grid square will occur. Listen to a few passes to get the timing down, and then try your best to initiate a contact. There will be pauses between contacts where you should break in with your callsign and grid square.

Summary

Amateur radio satellites are just like repeaters, but in space! Just like repeaters, they operate using split transmit and receive frequencies, and PL tones. Unlike repeaters, they generally utilize a smaller transmit power than your HT, and cover a much greater area. You can make a contact that's a few hundred or even a thousand miles away through an amateur radio satellite with nothing but a special antenna and your HT. Making these contacts is tricky, however, as you'll need to track the satellite across the sky with your antenna.

If everything goes well, you have just made your first long-distance contact! Some satellites support digital modes where you can transmit short strings of text with your location. Your HT does not support such activities, but slightly more expensive HTs do. If you've enjoyed satellite communications, you can consider creating a fixed antenna specifically for that purpose. Without a motorized ground station to track satellites, you will have to sacrifice directional gain in a fixed installation, but you can still achieve decent results.

Another interesting thing you can do with the hardware you already have is monitor a satellite pass with your software-defined radio. You can set up the antenna in a similar fashion to what was needed for the weather satellites chapter; you will need to adjust the length of the elements to match the desired frequency. You can also connect the SDR to your log-periodic antenna with the SMA cable.

In the next chapter, we'll discuss yet another way to use your amateur radio license: volunteer opportunities. Additionally, we'll talk about other radio topics that don't fit well into the rest of the text but are still interesting.

CHAPTER 10

Ham Nets, Volunteering, and More

The *amateur radio net* (used in this context as short for the word "network") is how groups of hams communicate with one another. Having every ham try and talk at the same time would be madness for large groups, so organizational structures exist that facilitate communications both in times of duress and for general communications. In this chapter, we'll explore amateur radio nets, and help you make your first ground-based contact.

We'll also explore further uses of your amateur radio license and how you can get involved in the amateur radio community, such as through volunteering. The radio technology itself may be interesting, but what makes this hobby so fun is the people you get to interact with and the interesting applications of radio.

Lastly, we'll discuss more radio-related topics that don't fit well into other chapters, and provide next steps for the continuation of your radio education!

© Alex Wulff 2019
A. Wulff, *Beginning Radio Communications*,
https://doi.org/10.1007/978-1-4842-5302-1_10

Making Contacts

You may have now successfully made contact with other hams through a satellite; however, this platform is not great for extended conversations. Part of the fun of amateur radio is talking with other individuals around you and having a long conversation. Hams will often engage in a *rag chew*, which is simply a long and enjoyable talk on amateur frequencies with one or more other operators. You can talk about basically anything—your setup, the other's signal, the weather, amateur radio in the area, and so much more. If you hear an individual once in your area, chances are you'll hear them again. Such conversations are not conducted through satellites but instead through ground-based repeaters or direct radio contact.

The spirit of amateur radio is cooperation, education, and fun, so avoid talking about contentious and divisive issues. Hams generally try to avoid politics and religion in particular—if you feel that a conversation is heading in that direction, then make sure to keep it civil and redirect it to another topic.

Amateur Radio Nets

Many single repeaters—or systems of repeaters—host recurring nets. As described above, nets are coordinated ways to talk with other hams, pass traffic, or buy and sell radio equipment. They also help coordinate communications in the event of an emergency or in the context of a large volunteer event. Some nets are scheduled—many occur weekly, biweekly, or daily at specific times. Other nets are set up for a predetermined purpose, such as a volunteer event. Nets are a fantastic way to hear how hams communicate with one another and behave on the air.

What makes a net a net is some form of structure. This can range from everything from an individual coordinating some traffic to an entire team of operators directing hundreds of hams. A common denominator of most nets is *net control*, or some individual/group that's "in charge." Net control is responsible for ensuring smooth operation of the net and resolving any problems that might crop up. In the case of most casual nets that you'll find on a repeater, net control will likely be an individual facilitating discussion, check-ins, and the passing of messages. You can identify nets in your area via an online search of something along the lines of "amateur radio nets around _____."

If you have the time of a particular net, and you know the frequency of the repeater that's hosting it, you should be good to go! Set up your radio, and tune in at the given time. The net control operator will likely start by announcing the name of the net and then ask for check-ins. At this point, amateur radio operators listening to the net will go around and announce their callsign and name. Some also indicate the hardware used for transmission, such as "mobile" for a car-based system or "handheld" for an HT-based contact.

The net control operator would then proceed down the list of individuals checked in, indicating when a given ham can talk. This ham can share information, talk about equipment that he or she has for sale, or simply talk about how his or her day is going!

Since repeaters utilize higher transmit powers than your HT, it can certainly be possible that you can hear a repeater, but the repeater cannot hear you. If you know that there's going to be a net on a repeater somewhere close to you, it can still be interesting to listen to the net, even if you can't reach the repeater with your signal.

Volunteering

A common practical use of amateur radio nets is for large events, such as the Head of the Charles Regatta, as shown in Figure 10-1. You'll find that at the heart of many large events lie amateur radio operators. Event coordinators will arrange for sometimes hundreds of hams to be present to help relay messages and coordinate traffic.

Figure 10-1. *Volunteers preparing for the 2019 Head of the Charles Regatta*

This event, which is the largest regatta in the world by number of boats, utilizes amateur radio operators to assist with communications. Some hams operate on boats on the Charles River (near Boston) to help with rescues and forward information. Other amateur radio volunteers are paired with medical teams or operate by themselves.

Communicating with cell phones during such events would be impractical, as it would take an extremely long time to disseminate messages across an event, and bottlenecks can occur where many people try and call one person. Commercial radio systems, which are essentially advanced networks of walkie-talkies, are utilized for many events. However, these systems are only effective for smaller groups of people and at limited ranges.

This leaves amateur radio as an efficient and convenient way to pass messages and keep event officials informed. Common events where you'll find amateur radio operators include marathons, large fairs/festivals, and other large public sporting events. Volunteering at such events is a fun way to watch the event and hone your amateur radio skills at the same time. As a communications volunteer, you'll get inside access to many areas of an event that regular volunteers cannot access, such as the finish line of large races.

Hams at such events fill many different roles. Experienced amateur radio operators with years of volunteer experience can operate net control. These individuals tightly control the various nets utilized by hams and ensure that messages get where they need to go. Net control is responsible for ensuring that hams do what they're supposed to.

All other hams are out in the field performing various duties. Some act as monitors, roaming around an event searching for abnormalities. If they detect a concern, these individuals immediately report it to net control and await further instruction. Hams can also serve as the communications link between volunteer teams. Teams of medical staff will oftentimes have an amateur radio operator with them to relay messages. Many important event officials also have a dedicated amateur radio operator with them— these officials are very busy, so passing on the burden of communications frees them to complete other tasks.

Volunteer events are also a great way to practice amateur radio skills in a disaster-like scenario. Some events can be chaotic, and many events result in injuries that need communicating. The Boston Marathon uses amateur radio operators to help coordinate the activities of hundreds of medical personnel. In a typical race, there can be over a thousand injuries that require treatment. Operating a radio in such an environment can be both challenging and fun.

Interesting VHF and UHF Signals

You might be a little underwhelmed with your radio if you can't reach any repeaters, but not to fear! There are plenty of interesting signals in the frequency range of your radio that you can listen to. In fact, your BaoFeng can tune to signals well outside of the amateur 2 m and 70 cm bands, although it is likely illegal to transmit at these frequencies. The following are some interesting things to listen to with your radio.

NOAA Weather Radio

NOAA, the same government agency that operates the satellites that we received images from in a previous chapter, operates a network of radio transmitters across the United States. These transmitters send out general weather information and warnings—the coverage of the transmitters is excellent, with all but the least densely populated areas of the country able to receive at least one station. A regional coverage map is shown in Figure 10-2. White areas have reliable coverage, while brown areas do not. Areas without coverage on the borders of the map are actually covered by transmitters not shown on the map (e.g., so there is coverage in Eastern Massachusetts).

Figure 10-2. A regional coverage map of NOAA weather radio in Eastern New York

Stations generally transmit around 162 MHz, with adjacent stations selecting frequencies that do not interfere with each other. You can identify stations around you by going to www.nws.noaa.gov/nwr/Maps/. Select your state, and then select the transmitter closest to you. Areas in white are areas with coverage. Selecting the station closest to you will give you the strongest signal, but it's definitely possible to listen to other stations that

201

are farther away. If you don't live in the United States, your government likely offers a similar service. There's also a lot of spillover of NOAA stations into Canada and Mexico, as the stations have transmit powers in the hundreds of watts.

Police/Fire/EMS Radio

Surprisingly enough, many public safety communications are completely unencrypted, and totally available for you to listen to via your HT. Most systems operate utilizing a similar repeater network to amateur radio repeaters. Systems will have a high-powered transmitter at a base station, and mobile units' communications will be picked up and rebroadcast by this repeater. This also makes it easier for you to monitor communications, as the transmissions are broadcast over wide areas.

You can monitor communications from the police, fire departments, ambulances, and just about any other public safety service that utilizes radios. These frequencies typically lie in the range of 450-460 MHz. If you look at that section of the US frequency allocation chart shown in Figure 10-3, you can see that these frequencies are designated as "land mobile," which makes sense considering these are generally car-mounted radios. Many other countries operate on similar frequencies. RadioReference.com has a great database of the frequencies used in various municipalities—you can find it here: www.radioreference.com/apps/db/.

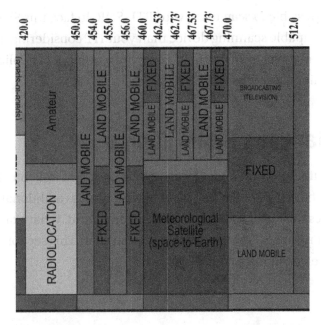

Figure 10-3. *The slice of the US frequency allocation chart from 420 MHz to 512 MHz. This selection includes both the aforementioned EMS frequencies and the 70 cm amateur radio band*

Scan Mode

There are likely all manner of communications filtering through the air waves around you that aren't listed anywhere online. Luckily, your radio has the ability to scan across various frequencies and stop if it finds anything interesting. BaoFeng HTs are by no means the fastest radio scanners available, but they get the job done. Select a frequency to start on, and then press and hold the "∗" key until your radio starts scanning. If it finds an active frequency, it will briefly pause on that frequency, determine if it's still active, and then continue scanning if nothing is found.

It's also possible to scan using your RTL-SDR. In fact, this SDR is a much more capable scanning device than your HT considering the greater processing capability available to it. There are a number of applications available online for this purpose.

Miscellaneous Radio Topics

There are numerous other uses for radio that do not fit well into the context of other chapters. In this section, we'll discuss additional radio-related topics that are important to the modern world. What exactly is radar? What makes 5G cellular networks so special? This section will answer these questions, and more.

Radar

While not explicitly radio communications, radar is still a fascinating subject that deals heavily in principles of electromagnetic radiation. At its core, radar is all about detecting things with radio waves. Radar is short for "radio detection and ranging." That is, radar systems are primarily designed to detect objects and pinpoint their position. Some radar systems also use the Doppler effect to measure the speed of an object.

The core of radar revolves around the principle of *reflection.* By sending out a pulse of energy and measuring the amount of time it takes for a reflection to come back to the radar system, one can determine how far away an object is. Radio waves travel at the speed of light, so the distance to an object is half the time it takes for the energy to go out and return to the radar multiplied by the speed of light.

In general, the larger an object is, the more energy it will reflect back. There exists a minimum amount of energy that an object must reflect back in order for it to be detected. If this quantity of reflected energy is too small, the energy from the object will be drowned out by noise and other reflections. The probability of detecting a given object is a function of the object's size, the distance to the object, and the amount of power sent out by the radar system, among other things.

Those wishing to avoid radar detection can only alter their appearance to a radar system, so much work is done by militaries to minimize the amount of energy that military planes and ships reflect. In fact, the odd shape of a modern military aircraft sometimes has as much to do with minimizing the object's appearance to radar as it does to improving aerodynamics. The F-35 fighter jet, shown in Figure 10-4, is a great example of this.

Figure 10-4. *The Lockheed Martin F-35 Lightning II*

A primary selling point of this aircraft is its ability to hide from enemy radar. The surfaces and paint of the jet are designed to scatter electromagnetic radiation or direct it away instead of directing it back to a radar array.

A radar array is comprised of many small antennas in a particular configuration. Lots of small antennas allow the operators of the radar system to create an extremely narrow and electronically steerable beam. A narrow beam means that the radar can tell operators where an object is to a greater degree of accuracy than with a wider beam. A good analogy of this is attempting to paint very fine details with a paintbrush as opposed to a can of spray paint. The spray paint can cover a larger amount of area, but it's not very precise.

The design of radar systems varies greatly depending upon their use. A common usage of radar is in military applications. Most missiles use radar to find their targets. All modern fighter jets have radar arrays in their noses. Practically every country monitors its airspace with radar installations. The list of radar in military applications is extensive. An interesting example is airliner-mounted radar arrays for surveillance purposes—see Figure 10-5.

Figure 10-5. The US Airborne Warning and Control System (AWACS). This is a jet-mounted radar array designed for ground and air surveillance. The large disk-shaped protrusion is the radar array

There are as many civilian uses for radar as there are military ones. If your car has adaptive cruise control (where your car automatically adjusts its speed to avoid hitting a vehicle in front of it), then it also has an integrated radar system. A car with adaptive cruise control utilizes radar to measure its distance to cars around it. This radar array allows for other interesting applications, such as front crash prevention.

5G

5G promises to revolutionize not only cellular communications, but also the modern technological world. An important way in which 5G improves upon existing 4G infrastructure is through enhanced mobile broadband (eMBB). Mobile broadband is simply cellular data services—every time you access the Internet through a cell tower instead of Wi-Fi, you're utilizing a mobile broadband service.

4G LTE supports real-world maximum data transfer rates of around 100 Mbps (million bits per second) in most places. As you can likely guess, eMBB greatly increases this figure. Real-world data transfer rates of over 1 Gbps (billion bits per second) are easily achievable with 5G hardware. This increase in speed comes mainly from the allocation of new parts of the electromagnetic spectrum for cellular data services.

4G generally utilizes frequencies between 500 MHz and 1 GHz. These frequencies still support decent data transfer rates, but also can propagate effectively across a large urban or rural environment. 5G will extend cellular communications into the range of tens of gigahertz. These are known as "millimeter-wave" bands, as the wavelength of such radio waves is on the order of millimeters or tens of millimeters. Higher-frequency electromagnetic waves support higher-frequency communications, which is primarily how 5G will achieve its remarkable increase in speed.

This increase in frequency comes at a cost, however. As mentioned throughout the text, radio waves with a frequency upward of a few gigahertz do not diffract well around obstacles. This means that an eMBB user will need to practically have a direct line of sight to an antenna. Cellular carriers need to install millimeter-wave antennas all over cities, and rural customers may never see millimeter-wave service.

5G will bring other benefits in addition to speed. The 5G standard can more effectively utilize existing spectrum, providing a speed increase for rural customers or customers without a millimeter-wave antenna near them. 5G also lowers communications latency and increases communications reliability, two items which are key to unlocking 5G's applicability in industrial and commercial applications.

LoRa

You've already got some exposure to using radio communications with microcontrollers in Chapter 6. The 2.4 GHz radios used in those exercises are great when you need a low-cost and short-range data link. However, this scenario only applies to a limited number of use cases. Many more situations require wireless communications across a longer range, for which different hardware and software is better suited. LoRa, short for long range, is such a system.

LoRa is a hardware specification that details a method for long-range and low-power data links for microcontroller-based devices.

Various radio modules utilize LoRa to connect devices across tens of kilometers, which is a much greater range than is achievable with the NRF24L01 module. Such a LoRa module is pictured in Figure 10-6.

Figure 10-6. *A LoRa radio module*

LoRa differs from other radio communications protocols in its usage of "chirps" for data transmission. A chirp is a special implementation of frequency modulation that yields interesting signal processing benefits. A single chirp is a signal that starts at one frequency and ends at another, increasing or decreasing linearly or nonlinearly with time. An "up-chirp" goes from a lower frequency to a higher frequency, whereas a down-chirp goes from a higher frequency to a lower frequency. LoRa utilizes a combination of different up and down chirps to encode information.

Chirps were originally used in radar applications to increase the probability of detecting a target. A chirp return from a target is much easier to identify and resolve from noise (after some special signal processing) than a return of a single frequency. Engineers determined that this same principle applies in the context of communications, and LoRa was born.

LoRa modules are relatively inexpensive (around $20 or $30) and are very easy to interface with various microcontrollers. They are a great next step if the section on radio communications with microcontrollers interested you. You can utilize LoRa for many remote sensing and control applications, including those with strict power requirements (such as battery-powered system). It is not suitable for transferring large amounts of data, however.

Satellite Internet and TV

Satellite communications have been a focus of many sections of this text, so it's important to mention the primary way in which consumers interact with satellites: satellite Internet and TV services. In some cities, satellites are the only reliable way to access the Internet due to a lack of ground-based infrastructure. Satellite Internet is a cost-effective option in such places, so aerial photos of many cities show satellite dishes dotting every roof. In Figure 10-7, you can see a dish adorning the roof of almost every structure.

Figure 10-7. *If you look closely, you can see hundreds of satellite dishes on the roofs of these buildings in Turkey*

The telecommunications satellites that serve these customers operate in geostationary orbit. A geostationary orbit is one in which the orbiting object appears to be fixed in the sky. This is only possible at a very particular altitude where the orbital velocity of the satellite exactly matches the rotational velocity of the surface of the Earth. Orbital velocity is a function of the altitude of the orbiting object, so only a very particular altitude is suitable. Simply put, geostationary satellites fall around the Earth at the same speed that the Earth turns. Geostationary satellites also must be directly above the equator, moving exactly parallel to the equator.

If the satellite were to move along any other trajectory, it would not orbit exactly "with" the Earth. Such satellites travel in a geosynchronous orbit, returning to the same place in the sky the same time every day. Geosynchronous and geostationary satellites orbit more than 20,000 miles above the surface of the Earth, or almost 100 times higher than the orbits of amateur radio satellites.

There are several benefits and drawbacks to having a satellite with such a high orbit. Since these satellites are so high up, they can be seen from almost every point on an entire continent. This allows satellite manufacturers to produce only one satellite to serve an entire country or region. The downsides to geostationary satellites' high altitude come in the form of transmit power and latency. Such satellites must transmit with kilowatts of power in order to have a usable signal down on Earth. Customers on Earth must also employ highly directional dishes to get their signals back up to the satellite. These dishes need to be precisely aligned, and occupy a lot of space.

Latency, or communications delay, is also a huge limitation of geostationary satellite communications networks. Geosynchronous orbit is over 20,000 miles away, a distance that radio waves take over a tenth of a second to traverse. Additionally, packets to and from satellite Internet users must pass through a supporting ground station for the satellite that adds additional latency. Network latency between a server located somewhat close to a client is generally less than 100 milliseconds, and often closer to 10–20 milliseconds. For a satellite Internet customer, this figure is often greater than 500 milliseconds. This high latency can have serious impacts on gaming, streaming, and many other Internet services.

Many space-based Internet companies are racing to deploy networks of satellites into LEO that can offer satellite Internet without high latencies or the need of a dish. These satellites are much closer to Earth, so it's easier and faster to send data back and forth from space to the ground. The challenging aspect of LEO satellite Internet networks is that many more satellites are needed to serve a region. At least one satellite must be overhead at all times in order for a consumer to access a company's network. This is only achievable by deploying a fleet of many satellites in carefully choreographed orbits. Network designs by SpaceX and Amazon call for thousands of satellites. These networks are much closer competitors to traditional broadband, as they offer similar latencies and speeds.

Radio Astronomy

Many of the largest radio dishes on Earth are not used for communications purposes. Such dishes are a specialized type of hardware known as radio telescopes. As you can likely guess from the name, radio telescopes are used for astronomical observation. An example of such telescopes is shown in Figure 10-8.

Figure 10-8. *The Effelsberg Radio Telescope. This telescope, located in Germany, has a diameter of 100 meters and started operation in 1972*

These dishes function in much the same way as optical telescopes—they collect electromagnetic radiation and focus it. Optical telescopes use optical lenses to focus light, whereas radio telescopes use parabolic reflectors to focus radio waves. Radio astronomy is somewhat more challenging than optical astronomy, however. Due to the longer wavelength of radio waves, the resolution of radio telescopes is much less than that of an optical telescope of the same size. Even a large telescope such as the one shown in Figure 10-8 does not have sufficient resolution to image faraway objects. To remedy this, astronomers use a technique called interferometry.

Interferometry is a way to boost the resolution of imaging systems by combining the data from multiple telescopes. The effective size of the combined telescope is that of the greatest distance between telescopes in the array. This offers huge benefits for astronomy, as it allows telescopes spaced all over the globe to be combined into one Earth-size telescope. This technique was utilized to capture the first ever picture of a black hole, as shown in Figure 10-9.

Figure 10-9. *The first-ever image of a black hole. Imaged using radio telescopes all over the globe, interferometry was instrumental in creating this picture. Astronomers captured radio waves with a wavelength of 1.3 mm to create this image. Credit: Event Horizon Telescope Collaboration*

Moving Forward and Closing

Now that you're well versed in a wide variety of radio-related topics, you can begin to focus your efforts on the things that interest you most. Radio technology is constantly evolving, so it's important to keep your skills sharp by learning and building. I can guarantee you that the best possible way to learn more about a subject is to create a project using that subject matter.

Radio technology is incredibly well suited to experimentation. Few other topics are as easy to learn by example—you may not be able to see radio waves directly, but myriad electronic interfaces allow you to observe how changes you make can affect a communications system.

One excellent place to further your knowledge of radio communications is in the realm of microcontrollers and Arduino. Microcontrollers enable you to create interesting and practical projects and learn while doing it. While you're still getting comfortable with the subject, you can find plenty of projects online that provide very detailed instructions. The best way to learn, however, is to create your own projects. By dreaming up an idea and creating the circuit yourself, you will learn much more than by following instructions. The possibilities for radio-related microcontroller projects are endless. Popular subject areas include the following:

- Radio-linked sensor networks

- Radio as a means of remote control for mechanical projects

- Radio telemetry from balloons, airplanes, and so on

- Radio for personal communications

- Novel uses of radio technology (using radio modems for something other than communications)

I also highly recommend getting more involved in the amateur radio community. Chances are, there's an amateur radio club around you that you can join. Experienced hams are perhaps the best resource for learning more about amateur radio and radio in general, so go out and find some!

If it's in your budget, I recommend purchasing better radio equipment. For a few hundred dollars, you can pick up a used amateur radio transceiver. These are non-portable tabletop devices that have a much higher transmit power than your HT and can operate on more bands. The filters on these devices are also much better than your BaoFeng radio, so you can expect much clearer voice transmissions (and you can hear weaker voice signals). You can also opt to purchase a higher-quality HT with better filters and more advanced functionality.

So far we've only operated using the FM voice mode, but there are tons of data modes to choose from. On lower-frequency bands, you can oftentimes find hams chatting using CW (Morse code) or SSB (a voice format that's a form of AM). Many computer-enabled digital modes exist, allowing for the transmission of text, voice, image, and more.

Regardless of how you decide to further your studies, never let radio and the electromagnetic spectrum cease to amaze you. Find something that piques your interest, and learn how it works. If you don't enjoy the process, then you're doing something wrong. Don't be afraid of failure, either. In the context of engineering, it's much easier to learn from failure than from success. Time spent pursuing something that doesn't work is not time wasted; rather, it is a valuable learning experience.

Index

© Alex Wulff 2019
A. Wulff, *Beginning Radio Communications*,
https://doi.org/10.1007/978-1-4842-5302-1

Printed in the United States
By Bookmasters